The Quest
for the
Original Text
of the
New Testament

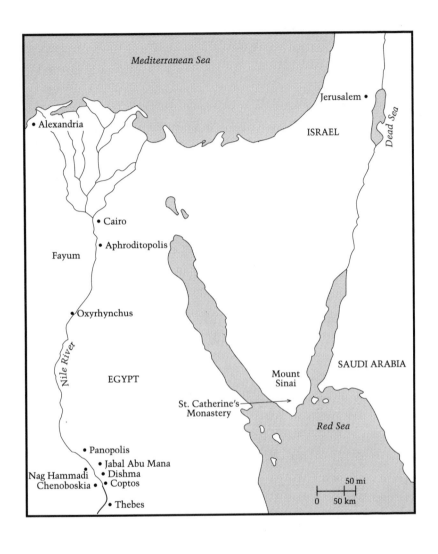

The Quest for the Original Text of the New Testament

Philip Wesley Comfort

BAKER BOOK HOUSE
Grand Rapids, Michigan 49516

Permission to reproduce the following papyri is gratefully acknowledged to
their owners:

𝔓1: The University Museum, University of Pennsylvania
𝔓5 and 𝔓13: The British Library, London
𝔓46: Department of Rare Books and Special Collections, University of
   Michigan Library
𝔓66 and 𝔓75: Foundation Bodmer, Geneva
𝔓69, 𝔓70, 𝔓71, 𝔓77, and 𝔓 90: The Committee of the Egypt Exploration
   Society

Library of Congress Cataloging-in-Publication Data

Comfort, Philip Wesley.
   The quest for the original text of the New Testament / Philip
Wesley Comfort.
      p.   cm.
   Includes bibliographical references and indexes.
   ISBN 0-8010-2566-4
   1. Bible. N.T. —Criticism, Textual. I. Title.
BS2325.C63   1992
225.7—dc20   92-477

This book is dedicated
to the memory
of those unnamed Christians
who made copies of the New Testament
and preserved, for us, the sacred text

Contents

Preface   9

Abbreviations   12

Chapter One
Introduction   13

Chapter Two
The Recovery of the Original Text
of the New Testament   19

Chapter Three
In Quest of the Original Text of the
New Testament   29

Chapter Four
Examining the Reliability of the Early Text   41

Chapter Five
Manuscripts Buried in Sand: The Oxyrhynchus
New Testament   59

Chapter Six
Papyri Hidden in Jars: The Chester Beatty Papyri ($\mathfrak{P}$45,
$\mathfrak{P}$46, $\mathfrak{P}$47) and the Coptos Papyri ($\mathfrak{P}$4, $\mathfrak{P}$64, $\mathfrak{P}$67)   71

Chapter Seven
Papyri from a Monastery Library: The Bodmer Biblical
Papyri ($\mathfrak{P}$66, $\mathfrak{P}$72, $\mathfrak{P}$75)   85

Chapter Eight
Textual Relationships among the Early Manuscripts:
A Book-by-Book Analysis   101

Chapter Nine
The Early Text Compared to the Nestle–Aland
Text (NA[26])   119

Chapter Ten
An Early Documentary Text
and Suggested Revisions for NA[26] and UBS[3]   129

Appendix
Textual Evidence for the Earliest Edition
of John's Gospel: Examining 𝔓5 and 𝔓75   157

Select Bibliography   167

Photographs   179

Author Index   191

Manuscript Index   193

Scripture Index   197

Preface

Preachers and teachers are famous for telling their congregations what a particular word means in the original Greek. For many years I was content to take their word for it. But then I had a strong desire to read, for myself, the New Testament in the original Greek. So I studied Greek, both Hellenistic and classical, and then enrolled in a class called the Greek New Testament. I was excited about reading the New Testament in the original text.

Prior to class we were asked to purchase a copy of the Greek New Testament (United Bible Societies, second edition), which I did. Then we were instructed to read the Gospel of Mark. I opened to the first page of the Greek text of Mark and began to read. But then I looked down at the bottom of the page and saw several technical notes concerning different readings in various manuscripts. "What's this?" I asked. "There is not one bona fide original Greek text. There are different readings from different ancient manuscripts?" That "got me going"—and until this day I have not stopped my quest for finding the original text of the Greek New Testament.

During this quest, I have come to believe that the history of the transmission (i.e., the process of copying) of the Greek text has several parallels with the history of the church. The church in the beginning was pure and glorious, then—generally speaking—went through a long period of corruption (during which time there was a small, faithful remnant who preserved the apostolic faith), then began to be recovered and restored. The

9

New Testament text from its inception was pure and untainted, then—generally speaking—went through a long process of textual corruption (during which time there were a few scribes who produced copies that preserved much of the original text), then began to be recovered and restored.

I mention this parallel because I have observed two conflicting views concerning the history of the transmission of the Greek New Testament. There are those who believe that the text was never corrupted and has never needed to be recovered. Unable to imagine that God would allow the text to become marred, they believe that God sovereignly preserved the original text in the majority of the manuscripts. They defend the fidelity of the Textus Receptus and/or what is called today the Majority Text. This is the text, they say, that the church preserved throughout the ages and is therefore the text that contains the original wording.

But the evidence of the early manuscripts speaks against this view, for the early manuscripts present a very different kind of text. Furthermore, not one of the early church fathers used the kind of Greek text that is found in the Textus Receptus or Majority Text. The Majority Text is a text supported by thousands of manuscripts dated from the fifth to the fourteenth centuries, but these manuscripts are basically replications of a fourth-century recension (produced by Lucian of Antioch) that incorporated hundreds (if not thousands) of textual changes in the New Testament text. This text does not present the original wording of the Greek New Testament.

Therefore, there are those who have another view about the history of the transmission of the Greek text. They see it in light of a recovery. They believe that the discovery of many early manuscripts in the past two centuries is an act of divine sovereignty because these manuscripts, being so much closer to the autographs, have provided the means for scholars to recover a purer form of the original text.

The concept of recovery is biblical. Adam fell into sin, and needed to be restored. Israel fell into idolatry, and needed to be recovered. Even the written Law was lost, and then was recovered by the high priest Hilkiah during the reign of Josiah. And so each recovery brings fresh joy and sweet contentment—for that which was lost becomes all the more precious when found.

Our joy comes from seeing a recovered New Testament text and appreciating the work of those archeologists, paleographers, and scholars who have searched for manuscripts in Egyptian ruins, deciphered the ancient texts, and studied the manuscripts to determine what the inspired New Testament authors originally wrote.

I am grateful to Al Fisher and Jim Weaver for their enthusiasm about this book. Maria den Boer, who coordinated the editorial work, was always a pleasure to work with, as was Dwight Baker who coordinated the design and photography in this book. The editor, David Aiken, did a superb job of perfecting this work.

ABBREVIATIONS

The abbreviations for specific manuscripts (such as $\mathfrak{P}$ for papyrus, as in $\mathfrak{P}75$) conform to those found in standard critical editions of the Greek New Testament (such as those listed below).

NA^{26} indicates Nestle–Aland's *Novum Testamentum Graece* (26th ed., 1979). UBS^3 indicates the United Bible Societies' *Greek New Testament* (3rd corrected ed., 1983). The text of both these editions, which are essentially the same in wording, was the work of five textual scholars: Kurt Aland, Matthew Black, Carlo Martini, Bruce Metzger, and Allen Wikgren. The critical apparatus of each edition is quite different. In this book focus is often given only to the critical apparatus of NA^{26}, which is more exhaustive, and for convenience is often referred to as the work of Aland (whose name appears on the title page with Nestle). Where both editions are being discussed, the work is often designated as NA^{26}/UBS^3. N^{25} designates the twenty-fifth edition of Nestle's *Novum Testamentum Graece* (1963).

Bibliographic citations are embedded in the text and abbreviated according to the date of writing and page numbers (e.g., Metzger 1971: 124). The full bibliographic data may be found in the bibliography on pp. 167–77.

Chapter One

INTRODUCTION

The pivotal period in early Christian history was the Diocletian persecution, followed by Constantine's acceptance of Christianity. Diocletian's belief that the old Roman religion would reinforce imperial unity formed the background to the persecution against the Christians. An edict issued at Nicodemia on February 23, 303, enjoined the demolition of churches and the burning of Christian books. This was the first Roman persecution that was designed not only to destroy Christians but to eradicate their sacred text, the New Testament.

Eusebius, the first church historian, witnessed the persecution and wrote of the many savage atrocities committed by the Romans against the Christians: "All this [persecution] has been fulfilled in our day, when we saw with our own eyes our houses of worship thrown down from their elevation, [and] the sacred Scriptures of inspiration committed to the flames in the midst of the markets" (*Ecclesiastical History* 8:2:1).

Those Christians most severely persecuted were living in Palestine, Egypt, and North Africa. Throughout the third century, Christians had secured permission from the government to purchase property and erect church buildings. These buildings were now demolished and the property confiscated. Church historian W. C. H. Frend writes (1984: 458):

No one in an official position in any part of the empire is recorded to have failed to carry out the emperor's orders. . . . All over the empire the authorities set about burning down Christian churches and collecting copies of the Scriptures. In proconsular Africa, for which there is good documentation, the first thing people knew of the emperor's orders was the sight of churches going up in flames.

Sadly, many Christians complied with the orders and handed over their copies of the Scriptures. However, there were those who kept their copies of the Scriptures from being destroyed. Some Christian leaders (such as Bishop Felix of Thibiuca) refused to hand over the Scriptures and suffered martyrdom as a consequence. Other Christian leaders fooled the authorities by handing over heretical works or medical books. Still others hid their texts.

In Africa, Alexandria was hit first and hardest. Bishop Peter fled from Alexandria to Oxyrhynchus. But the persecution followed him into rural Egypt. By the end of the third century we know that there were at least two Christian churches in Oxyrhynchus, one in the north and one in the south. These churches were very likely destroyed in the persecution under Diocletian (Winter 1933: 181). Need it also be said that many copies of the New Testament perished in the flames? But not all, for several second-century and third-century New Testament manuscripts have been discovered in Oxyrhynchus, all of which survived this persecution.

Entire (or nearly entire) Christian libraries escaped the Diocletian persecution. Two collections of biblical manuscripts, known today as the Beatty papyri and Bodmer papyri, were preserved from the flames. The Beatty manuscripts were hidden somewhere in the Fayum and the Bodmer in Abu Mana (see chaps. 6–7 below).

Hearing of the persecution in Alexandria and beyond, various Christians in rural Egypt would have done their best to remove New Testament manuscripts and other Christian writings from their churches and hide them in their homes, caves, or wherever else they could keep them from being confiscated by the authorities.

One Christian living in Coptos, Egypt, hid two treatises by Philo of Alexandria in a jar inside a hollow wall of his home. The codex had been stuffed with papyri fragments from Matthew and Luke. Very likely, the owner of this manuscript "concealed it with the intention of removing it from its hiding-place when danger had passed, either when Coptos was besieged and sacked by Diocletian in A.D. 292 or later in his reign during the last and severest of the persecutions" (Roberts 1979: 8).

In the North African city of Cirta (capital of Numidia), the mayor attempted to confiscate all the Scriptures from Bishop Paul. After searching the home where the Christians used to meet and finding only one copy of the Christian Scriptures, the mayor called upon Paul to tell where he had hidden other copies. Paul had been wise; the other copies had been taken to the homes of the readers (or lectors—those who read the Scriptures in church meetings) in that church. The wife of one of these readers handed over the books, and the house was searched to make sure there were no others (Frend 1984: 459; Stevenson 1957: 287–89).

In Abitina (in North Africa) the bishop handed over the Scriptures on demand. But his congregation disowned his act and carried on the church meeting in the home of the reader Emeritus. When the interrogators asked Emeritus to hand over his copies, he refused, saying he had "the Scriptures engraved on his heart." Others from Carthage shared the same sentiments. They all were imprisoned, but would never recant. Their attitude about the Bible (both Testaments) was steadfast: to alter a single letter of Scripture was sacrilegious and an insult to their author. It followed that to destroy the Testaments and divine commands of almighty God and the Lord Jesus Christ by handing them over to be burned merited lasting damnation in in-extinguishable fire (Frend 1984: 462).

We owe the preservation of the New Testament Scriptures to men such as Emeritus, a "reader" in his local church. In those days, the readers were responsible not only for reading Scripture during church meetings but also for keeping accurate and fresh copies of the Scriptures. They were the New Testament counterparts to the Old Testament Soperim and Masoretes. Some of them may have been scribes as well. For readers who were not scribes, it would have been their duty to have scribes make copies of the text for the church.

Furthermore, we very likely owe the preservation of the New Testament Scriptures themselves to the churches in rural Egypt, more than to the church in Alexandria, which was probably devastated by the Diocletian persecution. Of course, as is explained in later chapters, all of Egypt—not to mention the entire Greco-Roman world—had been influenced by Alexandrian scribal practices. (Thus, we owe the preservation of the original *wording* of the New Testament to the Alexandrian Christians.) Though it is possible that some New Testament manuscripts in Alexandria survived the persecution, it is likely that rural Egyptian churches preserved far more copies. Copies of the text may have been taken by Bishop Peter to Oxyrhynchus when he fled from Alexandria.[1] However, it is more likely that indigenous copies from Oxyrhynchus (i.e., copies made in Oxyrhynchus) and other rural towns in the Fayum or Upper Egypt (such as Coptos) were used by the Alexandrians after the persecution to provide archetypes for making new copies of the text. This hypothesis has backing in that certain Alexandrian manuscripts made after the age of Constantine (i.e., Codex Vaticanus and Codex Sinaiticus) are close copies of the kind of rural Egyptian manuscripts that survived the Diocletian persecution, for example, $\mathfrak{P}$4/64/67 (from Coptos), $\mathfrak{P}$13 (from Oxyrhynchus), $\mathfrak{P}$46 (from the Fayum), and $\mathfrak{P}$75 (from Abu Mana).

This book focuses on the manuscripts that made it through the Diocletian persecution—the New Testament manuscripts that had been made prior to this persecution, were hidden during it, and survived both its ravages and the destruction of time. Just as the members of the Qumran community hid their sacred Scriptures in jars in caves along the western shore of the Dead Sea to preserve them from the ravages of the Roman onslaught against the Jewish revolt of A.D. 132, so several early Christians hid their precious Scriptures in jars, homes, and caves to preserve them against the Roman persecution of 303. Those Jews never returned to recover their texts, nor did the Christians, whose manuscripts we now possess. These manuscripts were not rubbish or defective texts, nor were they castaway manu-

---

1. If the Alexandrian copies were to survive, even in Oxyrhynchus, they could not have been hidden in the places of assembly. In this regard, it is quite significant that none of the Oxyrhynchian manuscripts were discovered in any church buildings—because there are no remains of church buildings. Christians kept the manuscripts in their homes, and books of the New Testament were buried with other literary and nonliterary documents.

scripts destined for a genizah; they were the texts that the Christians wanted to use again after the persecution ceased. These early, extant manuscripts are the closest copies we have to the New Testament autographs, and they are the documents from which we can recover the original text of the New Testament.

Chapter Two

THE RECOVERY
OF THE ORIGINAL TEXT
OF THE NEW TESTAMENT

When I speak of the original text, I am referring to the "published" text—that is, the text in its final edited form as released for circulation in the Christian community. For some books of the New Testament, there is little difference between the original composition and the published text. After the author wrote or dictated his work, he (or an associate) made the final editorial corrections and then released it for distribution. As is the case for books published in modern times, so in ancient times the original writing of the author is not always the same as what is published—due to the editorial process. Nonetheless, the author is credited with the final edited text, and the published book is attributed to the author and considered the autograph. This autograph is the original published text.

Books such as Matthew, Luke, the pastoral Epistles, the general Epistles, and Revelation seem to have been produced in only one edition from the onset. But other books seem to have gone through two stages: a book was first written, edited, and published; afterward, it was reedited (redacted) and published afresh. This seems to be the case for books such as John (published first with twenty chapters and later with an appended chapter—see the appendix for discussion), Acts (published in two editions—one by Luke himself and another by an expander), and the Pauline Epistles (minus the pastoral Epistles).

The Pauline Epistles call for special consideration because they first circulated as individual works and then were later collected into a unified corpus. For a time, both forms of the Pauline Epistles could have been extant—as individual letters and as one corpus—until the latter outlived the former. Because it would be nearly impossible with books like John and the Pauline Epistles to distinguish between the first edition and the second edition, the second edition is considered the original text. (It is, however, possible to distinguish the first and second editions of Acts.)

Some scholars think it is impossible to recover the original text of the Greek New Testament because they have not been able to reconstruct the early history of textual transmission. For example, Robert Grant writes (1963: 51), "The primary goal of New Testament textual study remains the recovery of what the New Testament writers wrote. We have already suggested that to achieve this goal is wellnigh impossible." And Kenneth Clark says (1966: 15; repr. p. 118) that textual critics may be "pursuing the retreating mirage of the 'original text.'" Other modern scholars are less pessimistic, but are still quite guarded in affirming the possibility. I am optimistic because we have many early manuscripts of excellent quality and because our view of the early period of textual transmission has been getting clearer and clearer. I believe it is possible to recover the original text of the Greek New Testament.

When I speak of recovering the text of the New Testament, I am referring to individual books of the New Testament, not to the entire volume per se, because each book or group of books (such as the Pauline Epistles) had its own unique history of textual transmission. The earliest extant copy of an entire New Testament text is Codex Sinaiticus (written about 375). (Codex Vaticanus, written mid-fourth century, lacks the pastoral Epistles and Revelation.) Prior to the fourth century, the New Testament was circulated in its various parts: as a single book or a group of books. Manuscripts of individual books, dating from the late first century to the third century, have been found, for example, Matthew (𝔓1), Mark (𝔓88), Luke (𝔓69), John (𝔓5, 𝔓22, 𝔓52, 𝔓66), Acts (𝔓91), and Revelation (𝔓18, 𝔓47). Similar manuscripts containing groups of books have also been discovered, for example, the four Gospels with Acts (𝔓45 and perhaps 𝔓53), the Pauline Epistles (𝔓46), and the Petrine Epistles and Jude (𝔓72). Each of the books of the New Testament has had its own textual history and has been preserved with varying degrees of accuracy. Nonetheless, all of the books were altered from their original state due to the process of manual copying decade after decade, century after century. The text of each book needs to be recovered.

The recovery of the Greek New Testament has had a long history. The need for recovery arose because the New Testament text was affected by many variations in its early history. In the late first and early second centuries, the oral traditions and the written word existed side by side with equal status—especially with respect to the material of the Gospels. Often, the text was changed by scribes attempting to conform the written message to the oral tradition or to conform one Gospel account to another. By the end of the second century and into the third century many significant variant readings had entered into the textual stream.

The early period of textual transmission, however, was not completely marred by textual infidelity and scribal liberty. There were those scribes who copied the text faithfully and reverently—that is, they recognized that they were copying a sacred text written by an apostle or eminent church leader. The formalization of canonization did not ascribe this sacredness to the text. Canonization came about as the result of common, historical recognition of the sacredness of various New Testament books. Certain New Testament books, such as the four Gospels, Acts, and Paul's epistles were considered inspired literature from the onset. As such, certain scribes copied them with reverential fidelity, as is evident in certain early manuscripts (e.g., 𝔓1, 𝔓4/64/67, 𝔓23, 𝔓27, 𝔓35, 𝔓39, 𝔓46, 𝔓75, and 𝔓77).

Other scribes, however, felt free to make "improvements" in the text—either in the interest of doctrine and harmonization or due to the influence of a competitive oral tradition. The manuscripts produced in such a manner created a kind of "popular text," that is, an uncontrolled text. (This text type used to be called the "Western text," but scholars now recognize this as a misnomer.)

The first scribes to attempt a recovery of the original text lived in Alexandria, or at least they were familiar with Alexandrian scribal practices—for in the Hellenized world many appreciated the scholarly practices of Alexandria. Beginning as early as the second century, the Alexandrian scribes, whether associated with or actually employed by the scriptorium of the great Alexandrian library, and members of the scriptorium associated with the catechetical school at Alexandria (called the Didaskelion) were trained philologists, grammarians, and textual critics.

The Alexandrian Christian scribes must have emulated the kind of textual criticism begun by Aristotle (who classified manuscripts according to their date and value) and continued by Zenodotus, Aristophanes of Byzantium, and Aristarchus of Samothrace—all librarians in the great library at Alexandria. Zenodotus initiated the first scientific attempt to recover the original text of the Homeric poems. Aristophanes produced much-improved critical editions of Homer and other poets. Aristarchus is said to have been the founder of accurate literary scholarship. These learned men of Alexandria were the creators of scholarly philological criticism and textual criticism. Michael Grant states (1982: 259), "Their methods became canonical in determining the forms of book-production and literary analysis in all Hellenistic centers, and the earlier writings they had so carefully preserved and studied were handed down to the Romans, and thus to ourselves."

The Alexandrians were concerned with preserving the original text of literary works. Textual criticism was applied to Homer's *Iliad* and *Odyssey* because these ancient texts existed in many manuscripts. The scribes would make text-critical decisions concerning the original wording and then produce an archetype, a manuscript produced officially and deposited in the library. Whenever necessary, further manuscripts were copied from and collated against this archetype (Birdsall 1970: 312).

We can presume that the same kind of textual criticism was applied to the New Testament text by Christian scribes in Alexandria. From the second century to the fourth century, the Alexandrian scribes worked to purify the text from textual corruption. Speaking of their efforts, Günther Zuntz writes (1953: 271–72):

The Alexandrian correctors strove, in ever repeated efforts, to keep the text current in their sphere free from the many faults that had infected it in the previous period and which tended to crop up again even after they had been obelized [i.e., marked as spurious]. These labors must time and again have been checked by persecutions and the confiscation of Christian books, and counteracted by the continuing currency of manuscripts of the older type. None the less they resulted in the emergence of a type of text (as distinct from a definite edition) which served as a norm for the correctors in provincial Egyptian scriptoria. The final result was the survival of a text far superior to that of the second century, even though the revisers, being fallible humans, rejected some of its correct readings and introduced some faults of their own.

The Alexandrian type of text was perpetuated century after century in a few manuscripts, such as ℵ and B (fourth century), T (fifth century), Ξ (seventh century), L (eighth century), 33 (ninth century), 1739 (a tenth-century manuscript copied from a fourth-century Alexandrian manuscript), and 579 (thirteenth century). Unfortunately, most of the Alexandrian-type manuscripts disappeared for centuries—awaiting discovery fourteen to sixteen centuries later.

Concurrent with the Alexandrian text was the so-called Western text—which is better characterized as the popular text of the second and third centuries. In brief, this popular text was found in any kind of manuscript that was not produced by Alexandrian influences. This text, given to independence, is not as trustworthy as the Alexandrian text type. But because the Alexandrian text is known as a polished text, the Western text sometimes preserved the original wording. When a variant reading has the support of both Western and Alexandrian texts, it is very likely original; but when the two are divided, the Alexandrian witnesses more often preserve the original wording.

Near the beginning of the fourth century, another kind of Greek text came into being and then grew in popularity until it became the dominant text type throughout Christendom. This is the text type first instigated by Lucian of Antioch, according to Jerome (in the introduction to his Latin translation of the Gospels). Lucian's text was a definite recension (i.e., a purposely created edition)—as opposed to the Alexandrian text type, which came about as the result of a process wherein the

Alexandrian scribes, upon comparing many manuscripts, attempted to preserve the best text (thereby serving more as textual critics than editors). Of course, the Alexandrians did some editing (what we would today call copyediting). The Lucianic text is the outgrowth and culmination of the popular text; it is "characterized by smoothness of language, which is achieved by the removal of barbarisms, obscurities, and awkward grammatical constructions, and by the conflation of variant readings" (Anon. 1974: 607). Lucian (and his associates) must have used many different kinds of manuscripts of varying qualities to produce a harmonized, edited New Testament text. The kind of editorial work that went into the Lucianic text is what we would call substantive editing.

Lucian's text was probably produced around the time of the Diocletian persecution (ca. 303)—either shortly before or soon thereafter. During this persecution many copies of the New Testament were confiscated and destroyed. Not long after this period of devastation, Constantine came to power and then recognized Christianity as the state religion. There was, of course, great need for copies of the New Testament to be made and distributed to churches throughout the Mediterranean world. Around 330, Constantine commissioned Eusebius to make fifty copies of the Scriptures to be used by the churches in Constantinople (Eusebius, *Life of Constantine* 4:36). Some scholars have conjectured that Codex Vaticanus and Codex Sinaiticus are survivors of these fifty copies. But this conjecture is unlikely, as is fully explained by F. F. Bruce (1988: 204):

> It has frequently been surmised that the Vatican and Sinaitic codices of the Greek scriptures (one of them, if not both) are survivors of this consignment. That is unlikely: apart from some indications that the Vatican codex may have been produced in Egypt, they are our two chief witnesses to what is called the Alexandrian text type, and there is no indication that this text type was current in Constantinople and its neighbourhood in the period following 330. . . . If a guess may be hazarded, it is more likely that the fifty copies exhibited the text of the recent edition of Lucian of Antioch (martyred in 312), the ancestor of the Byzantine or "majority" text. If they did, this would help to explain the popularity of this form of text in Constantinople and the whole area of Christendom under its influence from the late fourth century on, a popularity which led to its becoming in fact

the majority text and to its being called by many students nowadays the Byzantine text.

Furthermore, Lucian's text began to be propagated by bishops going out from the Antiochan school to churches throughout the east. Lucian's text soon became the standard text of the Eastern church and formed the basis for the Byzantine text. It is thus the ultimate authority for the Textus Receptus.

While Lucian was forming his recension of the New Testament text, the Alexandrian text was taking on its final shape. As mentioned earlier, the formation of the Alexandrian text type was the result of a process (as opposed to a single editorial recension). The formation of the Alexandrian text involved minor textual criticism (i.e., selecting variant readings from various manuscripts) and minor copyediting (i.e., producing a readable text). There was far less tampering with the Alexandrian text than the Lucianic, and the underlying manuscripts for the Alexandrian text type were superior to those used by Lucian. Perhaps Hesychius was responsible for giving the Alexandrian text its final shape, and Athanasius of Alexandria may have made this text the archetypal text for Egypt.

As the years went by, there were less and less Alexandrian manuscripts produced, and more and more Byzantine manuscripts manufactured. Very few Egyptians continued to read Greek (with the exception of those in St. Catherine's Monastery, the site of the discovery of Codex Sinaiticus), and the rest of the Mediterannean world turned to Latin. It was only the Greek-speaking churches in Greece and Byzantium that continued to make copies of the Greek text. For century after century—from the sixth to the fourteenth—the great majority of New Testament manuscripts were produced in Byzantium, all bearing the same kind of text. When the first Greek New Testament was printed (ca. 1525), it was based on a Greek text that Erasmus had compiled, using a few late Byzantine manuscripts. This printed text, with minor revisions, became the Textus Receptus. The name *Textus Receptus* is associated with the second printed edition of Elzevir's Greek New Testament (1633), which told the reader "you have the text, now received by all."

Beginning in the seventeenth century, earlier manuscripts began to be discovered—manuscripts with a text that differed from that found in the Textus Receptus. Around 1630, Codex

Alexandrinus was brought to England. An early fifth-century manuscript containing the entire New Testament, it provided a good, early witness to the New Testament text (it is an especially good witness to the original text of Revelation). Two hundred years later, a German scholar named Constantin von Tischendorf discovered Codex Sinaiticus in St. Catherine's Monastery (located near Mount Sinai). The manuscript, dated around 360–375, is one of the two oldest vellum (treated animal hide) manuscripts of the Greek New Testament. The earliest vellum manuscript, Codex Vaticanus, had been in the Vatican's library since at least 1481, but it was not made available to scholars until the middle of the nineteenth century. This manuscript, dated slightly earlier (350) than Codex Sinaiticus, has both the Old and New Testaments in Greek; the last part of the New Testament (from Heb. 9:15 onward, including Philemon and the pastoral Epistles) is missing. A hundred years of textual criticism has determined that this manuscript is one of the most accurate and reliable witnesses to the original text.

Other earlier and important manuscripts were discovered in the nineteenth century. Through the tireless labors of men like Tischendorf, Samuel P. Tregelles, and F. H. A. Scrivener, manuscripts such as Codex Ephraemi Rescriptus, Codex Zacynthius, and Codex Augiensis were deciphered, collated, and published.

As the various manuscripts were discovered and made public, a few scholars labored to compile a Greek text that more closely represented the original text than did the Textus Receptus. At first, scholars appended variant readings to the Textus Receptus; then they began to abandon the Textus Receptus. In 1707 John Mill of Oxford produced a critical edition of the Textus Receptus with an extensive critical apparatus and a thorough prolegomena that detailed several principles of textual criticism pertaining to genealogical method. Though he did not change the Textus Receptus, he laid the foundations for modern textual criticism. In the 1720s Richard Bentley (who saved Codex Alexandrinus from a fire in the Cottonian library) made extensive plans to publish a Greek text that would represent the text at the time of Origen (early third century). His plans to supplant the Textus Receptus, however, were not realized because he never published his Greek text. A collaborator of Bentley's named Johann Jakob Wettstein did publish a Greek New Testament (Elzevir's text) with a new critical apparatus. In the 1730s Johann Albert Bengel (known as the father of modern textual and philological studies in the New Testament) published a text that deviated from the Textus Receptus according to the evidence of earlier manuscripts.

In the 1800s certain scholars began to abandon the Textus Receptus. Karl Lachmann, a classical philologist, produced a fresh text (in 1831) that presented the Greek New Testament of the fourth century. Tregelles (self-taught in Latin, Hebrew, and Greek), laboring throughout his entire lifetime, concentrated all of his efforts in publishing one edition of the Greek text (which came out in six parts, from 1857 to 1872). His goal was "to exhibit the text of the New Testament in the very words in which it has been transmitted on the evidence of ancient authority" (Tregelles 1879: ii). Henry Alford also compiled a Greek text based upon the best and earliest manuscripts. In his preface to *The Greek Testament* (a multi-volume commentary on the Greek New Testament, the first volume of which was published in 1849), Alford said (1874: 76) he labored for the "demolition of the unworthy and pedantic reverence for the received text, which stood in the way of all chance of discovering the genuine word of God."

During this same era, Tischendorf was devoting a lifetime of labor to discovering manuscripts and producing accurate editions of the Greek New Testament. In a letter to his fiancée he wrote, "I am confronted with a sacred task, the struggle to regain the original form of the New Testament" (cited in Metzger 1968: 126). In fulfillment of his desire, he discovered Codex Sinaiticus, deciphered the palimpsest[1] Codex Ephraemi Rescriptus, collated countless manuscripts, and produced several editions of the Greek New Testament (the eighth edition is the best).

Aided by the work of previous text critics, two British scholars, Brooke A. Westcott and Fenton J. A. Hort, worked together for twenty-eight years to produce a volume entitled *The New Testament in the Original Greek* (1881). Along with this pub-

---

1. A palimpsest is a manuscript in which the original writing has been erased and then written over. Through the use of chemicals and painstaking effort, a scholar can read the original writing underneath the overprinted text. Codex Ephraemi Rescriptus had the sermons of Ephraem written over the New Testament text.

lication, they published in 1882 their theory (which was chiefly Hort's) that Codex Vaticanus and Codex Sinaiticus (along with a few other early manuscripts) represented a text that most closely replicated the original writing. They called this text the Neutral text. According their studies, the Neutral text described certain manuscripts that had the least amount of textual corruption. It is this text that Westcott and Hort relied upon in compiling their edition.

The nineteenth century was a fruitful era for the recovery of the Greek New Testament; the twentieth century, no less so. Those living in the twentieth century have witnessed the discovery of the Oxyrhynchus papyri, the Chester Beatty papyri, and the Bodmer papyri. To date, there are nearly one hundred papyri containing portions of the New Testament—several of which date from the late first century to the early fourth century. These significant discoveries, providing scholars with many ancient manuscripts, have greatly enhanced the effort to recover the original wording of the New Testament.[2]

At the beginning of the twentieth century, Eberhard Nestle used the best editions of the Greek New Testament produced in the nineteenth century to compile a text that represented the majority consensus. The work of making new editions was carried on by his son Erwin for several years, and it is now under the care of Kurt Aland. The latest edition (the 26th) of Nestle–Aland's *Novum Testamentum Graece* appeared in 1979 under the leadership of Kurt Aland and Barbara Aland (followed by several corrected printings). The same Greek text appears in another popular volume published by the United Bible Societies, the *Greek New Testament* (third edition in 1975, a corrected printing in 1983). The twenty-sixth edition of the Nestle–Aland text is regarded by many as representing the latest and best in textual scholarship. But the question remains: Does it represent the original text of the Greek New Testament?

2. Some of the preceding paragraphs were adapted from my 1991 book, *Complete Guide to Bible Versions.*

Chapter 3

In Quest
of the Original Text
of the New Testament

In their 1987 book, *The Text of the New Testament* (p. 24), Kurt and Barbara Aland argue that the text printed in both the twenty-sixth edition of Nestle–Aland (NA[26]) and the third edition of the *Greek New Testament* (UBS[3]) "comes closer to the original text of the New Testament than did Tischendorf or Westcott and Hort, not to mention von Soden." And in several other passages they intimate that this text may very well be the original text. This is evident in Kurt Aland's defense (1981: 274–75; translation from Epp 1980: 149–50) of NA[26] as the new "standard text":

> The new "standard text" has passed the test of the early papyri and uncials. It corresponds, in fact, to the text of the early time. . . . At no place and at no time do we find readings here [in the earliest manuscripts] that require a change in the "standard text." If the investigation conducted here in all its brevity and compactness could be presented fully, the detailed apparatus accompanying each variant would convince the last doubter. A hundred years after Westcott–Hort, the goal of an edition of the New Testament "in the original Greek" seems to have been reached. . . . The desired goal appears now to have been attained, to offer the writings of the New Testament in the form of the text that comes nearest to that which, from the hand of their

authors or redactors, they set out on their journey in the church of the 1st and 2d centuries.

First of all, the Alands should be applauded for speaking about recovering the *original* text, for it is apparent that many modern textual critics have given up any hope of recovering the original text. I think it can be recovered, and I think NA^{26}/UBS^3 is quite close to presenting the original text—but not completely. For, while the Alands present strong arguments for the early manuscripts as providing the best witness to the original text, NA^{26}/UBS^3 does not always follow the evidence of the early manuscripts (this point is fully developed in chap. 9). Of course, an "early" manuscript is not always the most trustworthy manuscript; nonetheless, several of the earliest manuscripts are the most reliable—a position constantly affirmed by the Alands.

The Alands point out (1987: 56–64) that there are over forty manuscripts that date before the beginning of the fourth century. However, their dating of certain manuscripts is too conservative, inasmuch as they date only one manuscript ($\mathfrak{P}$52) in the second century. (Most of the dating of the early papyri has been too conservative because Grenfell and Hunt did not believe the codex existed before the third century and therefore dated many Oxyrhynchus papyri in the third or fourth century—papyri that should have been dated in the second or third century.) In recent years, certain paleographers have assigned earlier dates to some New Testament manuscripts.

One of the most significant papyri is $\mathfrak{P}$46 (also known as Chester Beatty Papyrus II, usually dated around 200), which contains all of Paul's letters except the pastoral Epistles. In a very convincing article written in 1988, Young K. Kim dated $\mathfrak{P}$46 to the reign of Domitian (A.D. 81–96), mainly because all other literary papyri comparable to the handwriting style of $\mathfrak{P}$46 are dated in the first century A.D. and because there are no dated parallel papyri from the second or third centuries. If this dating is accurate, we have a copy of the Pauline corpus made within the same decade that the Pauline corpus is believed to have been assembled—that is, 75–85.[1] This dating of $\mathfrak{P}$46

---

1. Kim's dating has been affirmed by O'Callaghan 1988. It should be noted that the form of the upsilon in $\mathfrak{P}$46 follows a ductus common in the first cen-

greatly increases its importance, for it makes 𝔓46 the manuscript closest to its original. Even if Kim's dating is too early,
it strongly challenges the date of 200 usually assigned to 𝔓46.
At the least, one can say that 𝔓46 is late first century to early or
middle second century (85–150). And if this is the case, then
𝔓52 is still the earliest extant New Testament manuscript.

In the same article and in correspondence with me, Kim provides earlier dates for some other early New Testament manuscripts. Many paleographers would confirm the same dating for
several of these manuscripts, although several would be
inclined to add about another twenty-five years to those dated
in the second century.

The earliest manuscripts and their contents, with dates
assigned according to general scholarly consensus, are as follows:

𝔓52   a few verses of John 18, early second century (ca.
94–127). The editor of this manuscript, Colin H.
Roberts, made a thorough comparison (1935: 13–15)
of the manuscript with non-Christian papyri from
the end of the first century and the beginning of the
second century and then noted several marked similarities in letter forms (ligatures) to texts dated from
94 to 127. Because the final edited copy of John was
published around 85–95, 𝔓52 could be a first-
generation copy.

𝔓87   a few verses of Philemon, early second century (ca.
125) (the handwriting of 𝔓87 is very similar to that
found in 𝔓46)

𝔓77   a few verses of Matthew 23, middle second century
(ca. 150)

𝔓45   (also known as Chester Beatty Papyrus I) portions
of all four Gospels and Acts, middle second century
(ca. 150)

---

tury A.D. However, one should be cautious about dating this manuscript on
this basis alone because it is possible that the scribe of 𝔓46 deliberately
archaized the script. Metzger (1991: 265) provides further cautions against
accepting a date for 𝔓46 around 80. He argues that "it must have taken some
time for the nine epistles that are preserved in 𝔓46 to have been collected, then
a copy made of the corpus (the archetype), and finally a copy of this to reach
the interior of Egypt."

𝔓32	portions of Titus 1–2, third quarter of the second century (ca. 175)
𝔓90	a portion of John 18–19, third quarter of the second century (ca. 175)
𝔓4/64/67	portions of Matthew and Luke (ca. 200) (these three papyri belong to one manuscript of excellent quality—see the discussion in chap. 6)
𝔓1	Matthew 1 (ca. 200)
𝔓13	Hebrews 2–5 and 10–12 (ca. 200)
𝔓27	a portion of Romans 8–9 (ca. 200)
𝔓66	(also known as Bodmer Papyrus II) most of John, ca. 200 (but dated in 1960 by Herbert Hunger, director of papyrological collections in the National Library at Vienna, to ca. 125–150)
𝔓48	a portion of Acts 23, early third century (ca. 220)
𝔓75	(also known as Bodmer Papyrus XIV/XV) most of Luke and John, early second century (ca. 150–200)

In addition to these early papyrus manuscripts, there is another late second-century vellum manuscript: 0189, containing a portion of Acts 5. There are thirty-one third-century manuscripts, with portions from the passages noted below:

𝔓5	John 1, 16, 20
𝔓9	1 John 4
𝔓12	Hebrews 1
𝔓15	1 Corinthians 7–8
𝔓16	Philippians 3–4 (𝔓15 and 𝔓16 are parts of the same manuscript)
𝔓18	Revelation 1
𝔓20	James 2–3
𝔓22	John 15–16
𝔓23	James 1
𝔓28	John 6
𝔓29	Acts 26
𝔓30	1 Thessalonians 4–5, 2 Thessalonians 1
𝔓35	Matthew 25
𝔓37	Matthew 26
𝔓38	Acts 18–19
𝔓39	John 8
𝔓40	Romans 1–4, 6, 9

𝔓47	Revelation 9–17
𝔓49	Ephesians 4–5
𝔓53	Matthew 26, Acts 9–10
𝔓65	1 Thessalonians 1–2
𝔓69	Luke 22
𝔓70	Matthew 2–3, 11–12, 24
𝔓72	1–2 Peter, Jude
𝔓78	Jude
𝔓80	John 3
𝔓92	Ephesians 1, 2 Thessalonians 1
0162	John 2
0171	Matthew 10, Luke 22
0212	a Diatessaron manuscript containing small portions of each Gospel
0220	Romans 4–5

The manuscripts listed above, especially the first group (those dated before the early third century), provide the source for recovering the original text of the New Testament. Many of these manuscripts are over two hundred years older than the two great manuscripts discovered in the nineteenth century: Codex Vaticanus (ca. 350) and Codex Sinaiticus (ca. 360). These two manuscripts revolutionized New Testament textual criticism in the nineteenth century and were the impetus for the compilation of new critical editions of the Greek New Testament by men such as Tregelles, Tischendorf, and Westcott and Hort.

Tregelles, working according to principles similar to Karl Lachmann's, compiled a text based on the evidence of the earliest manuscripts. Tischendorf attempted to do the same, even though he was too biased toward his prized discovery, Codex Sinaiticus. Westcott and Hort implemented the same principle when they created their critical edition, even though they were biased toward Codex Vaticanus. Nonetheless, Westcott and Hort made an attempt to print the original text of the Greek New Testament.

Many critics in this century deride their or anyone else's making such an attempt because they are convinced that it is impossible to recover the original text due to the great divergence of readings that exist in so many different manuscripts and the inability to reconstruct a history of the early text. Other critics have argued that it is not wise to base a recovery of the original text on manuscripts that are all Egyptian in origin.

Eldon Epp correctly recognizes that the early papyri provide the key to unlocking the recovery of the original text of the New Testament. However, he hesitates to lay hold of that key because he has some concerns about the fact that all the early papyri have come from Egypt. Epp asks some penetrating questions (1989b: 104–5):

> How representative, really, of the earliest history of the NT text are these earliest papyri? What assurance do we have that these randomly surviving manuscripts represent in any real sense the entire earliest period of the text? Subsidiary questions appear: First, all of these documents come from one region, Egypt. Can we be satisfied with Egypt as the exclusive locale for viewing this earliest history of the text? Was Egypt in the third century A.D. representative of the NT text for *all* of Christianity at that period?

In response to Epp, I say "yes." The early papyrus manuscripts represent not only the Egyptian New Testament text, but also the text of the entire early church. Kurt Aland (1987) affirms this position by pointing out that (1) we are not sure if all of the papyri discovered in Egypt actually originated in Egypt and (2) that the text typically called the Egyptian text (as opposed to the Western or Byzantine text) is the text displayed in the writings of the early church fathers who lived outside of Egypt, for example, Irenaeus, Marcion, and Hippolytus. Therefore, it is likely that the manuscripts discovered in Egypt are typical of the text existing at that time throughout the entire church. Furthermore, Alexandria took the lead among all the Greco-Roman cities in scholarship and textual studies. Thus, its influence would have extended over the entire Mediterranean world.

It must be remembered that before the third century churches throughout the Mediterranean area were not isolated from one another. Due to a flourishing commerce, accessible highways, and open seaports (all under Roman rule), there was a regular flow of communication between Carthage, Rome, Alexandria, and Jerusalem. The churches in North Africa and Egypt were not isolated from the rest of the churches to the north. This connection began from the earliest days of the church. Some of the first to become Christians on the day of

Pentecost (30) were from Egypt and Libya (Acts 2:10); undoubtedly some of them returned home with the gospel. The Ethiopian eunuch, after receiving Jesus as his Savior, must have returned home with the gospel (Acts 8:25–39).

The earliest biblical indication of the presence of Christianity in Egypt is in Acts 18:24–25, where we are told that Apollos the Alexandrian "had been instructed in the way of the Lord [i.e., Jesus]" before coming to Ephesus. Some Western manuscripts (D and it[gig]) have an alternate reading: κατηχημένος ἐν τῇ πατρίδι τὸν λόγον τοῦ κυρίου (had been instructed in his own country in the word of the Lord). Even though this reading is not original, "the implication of the statement no doubt accords with historical fact" (Metzger 1971: 466) and thereby suggests that Christianity had come to Alexandria by 50. The text, even without the Western addition, implies that Apollos received Christian instruction before he came to Asia.

There must have been a church in Alexandria by the middle of the first century. Alexandria had a large Jewish population with connections to Jerusalem and Palestine. Thus, it would have been natural for the gospel to have been taken there soon after Pentecost (30) or during the first diaspora from Jerusalem (50; see Acts 11:19).

With respect to the early history of the New Testament text and New Testament textual criticism, no city is more important than Alexandria because this city had the facilities of scholarship and book production that were necessary for making accurate copies. The Ptolemies had established a museum and a library to enhance scholarship. Bell elaborates (1948: 53–54):

The Museum was primarily a temple of the Muses; in actual fact it was a combination of something like a modern academy and a university. Here were established a number of scholars, scientists, and literary men who enjoyed free board and lodging and were exempt from taxation. For their use the Ptolemies collected a vast library of books, which eventually contained something like half a million rolls. In order to enrich the collection Ptolemy III issued an order that all travellers disembarking at Alexandria must deposit any books contained in their baggage, which, if required, were taken by the Library, the owner receiving in exchange an official certified copy. . . . In the Library were founded the sciences of bibliography and textual criticism; catalogues of classical Greek literature were compiled, [and] the texts of Homer and other authors were cleansed of many corruptions and established in a form transmitted with comparatively little change to modern times.

The Alexandrian museum and library became the most influential place of scholarship in the Greco-Roman world. The Christians in Alexandria were influenced by this "university" when they formed their own school, the catechetical school (or Didaskelion). Bell (1953: 96) says that the principal motive for forming this school "was no doubt to provide for Christians a means of higher education other than that of the pagan university in the Museum." According to Eusebius, the catechetical school emphasized "the teaching of the sacred writings," combined with instruction in philosophy and science. This school also established a library, whose scribes would have been informed by the textual criticism practiced at the museum's library. Alexandrian textual criticism worked at ridding the text of textual corruption—not at providing recensions (i.e., edited texts).

The catechetical school must have been established in the early second century, if not earlier. Eusebius records its existence in his report of Pantaenus becoming head of the school in 160: "At that time a man named Pantaenus having a great reputation for his education was directing the way of life of the believers in Alexandria, for from ancient custom a school of sacred teachings had existed among them."[2] In 180 Clement, who took over the leadership when Pantaenus left Alexandria, worked hard "to establish the small catechetical school there as the center of Christian study and mission" (Frend 1984: 286). By 200 Clement had built up a flourishing community of well-educated Alexandrian Christians. But then, due to the savage persecution of 202, Clement fled Alexandria. Origen took over from Clement and established a well-known school of Christian scholars. Origen provided a link between Egypt and the regions north of the Mediterannean when he went to Caesarea in 231 and instituted a center of Christian scholarship. Origen brought

2. Eusebius, *Ecclesiastical History* 5:10; translation from Griggs 1990: 21. However, I would translate διδασκαλείου τῶν ἱερῶν λόγων as "a school of [for learning] sacred writings," which would include the Old Testament and New Testament.

his library with him and the wherewithal to establish a library and Christian scriptorium.

History also tells us that there were churches in the rural areas south of Alexandria as early as the first part of the second century. Several of the earliest New Testament manuscripts— those dating from the early second century (see list above)— have come from the Fayum and Oxyrhynchus, thereby revealing the existence of Christians in these rural towns as early as 110. This is the area where archeologists have discovered nearly all of our early New Testament manuscripts. No manuscripts have been found in Alexandria because the Alexandrian library was destroyed twice over (once, accidentally, by the Romans and another time, purposely, by the Muslims). Furthermore, the water table is too high in Alexandria; papyri could not withstand the moisture.

Rural Middle Egypt, because of its dry climate and low water table, is a repository of manuscripts produced indigenously and extra-locally. The extant manuscripts, I believe, present a fair sampling of what would have existed in the late first to third centuries throughout the entire Greco-Roman world. That is to say, if we could find—by some miracle—early manuscripts in Turkey, Israel, Syria, or Greece, they would very likely contain the same samplings of readings found in the so-called Egyptian manuscripts. In other words, the New Testament manuscripts used and read in the churches in Egypt during the early centuries of the church fairly represent what was being used and read throughout all the churches. Furthermore, it is safe to assume that rural Middle Egypt preserved many manuscripts that had come from Alexandria (or were prepared in the Alexandrian tradition) and other cities, such as Rome or Antioch. Paleographer E. G. Turner (1968: 51) mentions the possibility that "religious books, Latin or Greek, found in Egypt were the product of scriptoria outside Egypt."

Rural Middle Egypt was not isolated from the rest of the world. Numerous nonliterary papyri discovered there show regular communication between the Fayum and Alexandria, Carthage, and Rome. This communication included general correspondence about works of literature and scriptoral practices. Therefore, among those who produced the early manuscripts we have today, there must have been some scribes who were producing copies of New Testament books, much in the same manner as those who lived elsewhere in the Greco-Roman world.

The manuscripts discovered in Egypt are the ones from which we can reconstruct the original text of the Greek New Testament. At the end of the twentieth century, we are in a far better position to do this than those in the nineteenth century because we have many more earlier manuscripts to work with than they did.

But there are those who say it is too simplistic to think that the earliest manuscripts are the best manuscripts. These scholars argue that the original reading can be found in any manuscript of any date. This is hypothetically true, but hardly bears up when put into practice. A reading with testimony from one early papyrus manuscript of reputed reliability (with the support of at least one other early reliable Greek manuscript) is far more likely to represent the original text than a reading found in later manuscripts.

Textual critics working with ancient literature universally acknowledge the supremacy of earlier manuscripts over later ones. Textual critics of classical literature would love to have the same kind of early witnesses that we possess. In fact, many of them work with manuscripts written one thousand years after the autographs were composed. The Dead Sea Scrolls provide a text that is nearly eight hundred years closer to the originals than medieval Masoretic manuscripts; yet many of the Dead Sea manuscripts are still six hundred to eight hundred years removed from the time of composition. New Testament textual critics have a great advantage.

Nineteenth-century New Testament textual scholars—such as Lachmann, Tregelles, Tischendorf, and Westcott and Hort—worked on the basis that the earliest witnesses are the best witnesses. We would do well to continue this approach to recovering the original text. Textual scholars since the time of Westcott and Hort have been less inclined to produce editions based on the theory that the earliest reading is the best. Most present-day textual critics are more inclined to endorse another maxim: that reading is most likely original that best explains the variant readings.

This maxim (or "canon" as it is sometimes called), as good as it is, produces conflicting results. For example, two scholars, using this principle to examine the same variant, may not agree. One might argue that the variant was produced by a copyist attempting to emulate the author's style; the other could claim the same variant has to be original because it accords with the author's style. Or, one might argue that a variant was produced by an orthodox scribe attempting to rid the text of a reading that could be used to promote heterodoxy or heresy; another might claim that the same variant has to be original because it is orthodox and accords with Christian doctrine (thus a heterodoxical or heretical scribe must have changed it). Furthermore, this principle allows for the possibility that the reading selected for the text can be taken from any manuscript of any date. This can lead to subjective eclecticism.

Modern textual scholars try to temper the subjectivism by employing a method called "reasoned eclecticism." According to Michael Holmes (1989: 55), "Reasoned eclecticism applies a *combination* of internal and external considerations, evaluating the character of the variants in light of the MSS evidence and vice versa in order to obtain a balanced view of the matter and as a check upon purely subjective tendencies." The Alands favor the same kind of approach, calling it the "local-genealogical method." In the introduction to NA[26] (p. 43*), they define it as follows:

> It is impossible to proceed from the assumption of a manuscript stemma, and on the basis of a full review and analysis of the relationships obtaining among the variety of interrelated branches in the manuscript tradition, to undertake a *recensio* of the data as one would do with other Greek texts. Decisions must be made one by one, instance by instance. This method has been characterized as eclecticism, but wrongly so. After carefully establishing the variety of readings offered in a passage and the possibilities of their interpretation, it must always then be determined afresh on the basis of external and internal criteria which of these readings (and frequently they are quite numerous) is the original, from which the others may be regarded as derivative. From the perspective of our present knowledge, this local-genealogical method (if it must be given a name) is the only one which meets the requirements of the New Testament textual tradition.

The local-genealogical method assumes that, for any given variation unit, any manuscript (or manuscripts) may have preserved the original text. Applying this method produces an extremely uneven documentary presentation of the text. For example, in one verse with four variation units, the text can be drawn from 𝔓45 (vs. 𝔓75, ℵ, and B) in the first unit, from 𝔓75 (vs. 𝔓45, B, and ℵ) in the second unit, from ℵ (vs. 𝔓45, 𝔓75, and B) in the third unit, and from B (vs. 𝔓45, 𝔓75, and ℵ) in the fourth unit. Anyone studying the critical apparatus of NA[26] will detect that there is not an even documentary presentation. The eclecticism is dispersed throughout the text.

Both reasoned eclecticism and the local-genealogical method tend to give priority to internal evidence over external evidence. But it has to be the other way around if we are going to recover the original text. This was Westcott and Hort's opinion. With respect to their compilation of *The New Testament in the Original Greek*, Hort wrote (1882: introduction p. 17), "Documentary attestation has been in most cases allowed to confer the place of honour as against internal evidence."

In this respect, Westcott and Hort need to be revived. Ernest Colwell was of the same mind when he wrote "Hort Redivivus: A Plea and a Program" in 1968. In this article (p. 135), Colwell decries the "growing tendency to rely entirely on the internal evidence of readings, without serious consideration of documentary evidence." Colwell calls upon scholars to attempt a reconstruction of the history of the manuscript tradition. But very few scholars have followed Colwell's urgings because they believe (as do the Alands, noted above) that is impossible to reconstruct a manuscript stemma for the Greek New Testament. They say this because they fear that someone will attempt to make a stemma back to the original, and such a reconstruction will involve a subjective determination of the best line of manuscripts. Westcott and Hort have been accused of doing this when they created the "Neutral" text, leading from B back to the original. However, a reconstruction of the early manuscript tradition does not necessarily mandate a genealogical lineage back to the original text—although that is the ultimate purpose of making a stemma. The reconstruction can help us understand the relationships between various manuscripts and provide insights into origination and associations (see chap. 8). In the process, it might also be discovered that, out of all the extant manuscripts, some of the earliest ones are, in fact, the closest replicas of the original text.

Chapter Four

EXAMINING
THE RELIABILITY
OF THE EARLY TEXT

S ome textual critics argue that an early date for a New Testament manuscript is not necessarily all that significant because they believe the early period of textual transmission was inherently free. Those who espouse this view argue that the scribes making copies of various books of the New Testament prior to the period of canonization (late third century) used liberty in making their copies. The Alands (1987: 69) go so far as to say that early Christian scribes felt free to make changes because they "considered themselves filled with the Spirit." Unlike the Jewish scribes who meticulously made accurate copies of the sacred Old Testament text, the Christian scribes have been characterized as not feeling obligated to produce exact copies of their exemplars because they had not yet recognized the "sacredness" of the text they were copying.

This view of the early period, which has become common among New Testament textual critics, is not entirely true, because many of the early Christian scribes were cognizant of their Judeo-Hellenistic literary tradition. They would have transferred the Jewish sacred regard for the Old Testament Scriptures to the New Testament Scriptures, and they would

41

have applied the Hellenistic appreciation for preserving the original wording of literary works to the New Testament texts. Furthermore, there is evidence that, as early as 70, Christian scribes throughout the Greco-Roman world followed certain standard scriptoral practices in producing copies of New Testament books.

The writers of these New Testament books were Jews who believed that the Old Testament—in Hebrew and in Greek— was the inspired Word of God. (The one Gentile among the writers, Luke, was both an educated Hellenist and a companion of Jewish Christians.) Because of their Jewish background, they had great respect for the Scriptures, which had become central to their worship and religious life. They were the people of the book. Most of them read the Greek Old Testament, the Septuagint, which was very likely the translation work of Alexandrian Jews. When the New Testament writers quoted the Scriptures, they usually cited the Septuagint. And when Paul said that "all Scripture is God-breathed and is useful for teaching, rebuking, correction, and training in righteousness," he was speaking of the Septuagint, which Paul encouraged Timothy to read out loud to the believers in church assemblies (see 2 Tim. 3:15–17). Concerning the Christians' respect for the Septuagint, C. H. Roberts writes (1970: 50):

> For the earliest Christians [the Septuagint] was both a datum of their religious life and a model for what in course of time became the New Testament. With this attitude went a concern for preserving the precise wording of the translated text; the Jewish rule that the sacred books must be read, not recited after being learnt by heart (as was the case with the uncanonised oral Law), itself contributed to the safeguarding of the text. The Church knew no such ban, but the general attitude to the sacred writings whether of the old or of the new dispensation was much the same.

Several of the early papyri containing portions of the Septuagint demonstrate that the early Christians took great care in making accurate copies of the sacred text. For example, the Chester Beatty Numbers–Deuteronomy codex (late first century A.D.), composed by a Christian scribe, displays the marks of a corrector and other reading aids. Roberts (1979: 22) says that this "scrupulous reproduction of the text may be a legacy from Judaism and reminds us that . . . the quality of book production [goes] hand in hand with quality of text."

The same kind of textual fidelity displayed in copies of the Septuagint is also manifest in various copies of the New Testament. Often, the same Christian scribes worked on both; and, often, copies of both the Septuagint and the New Testament were retrieved from ancient Christian libraries—as in the case of the Oxyrhynchus papyri and Chester Beatty papyri.

Jewish Christian scribes would have emulated Jewish scribal practices. This began with the making of copies of the Septuagint, which they believed was an inspired text, and would have extended to any New Testament book they regarded as authoritative or inspired or both. Christians would have been aware of the strict rules that governed the copying of the Old Testament text and the reverence given to the copies. Of this strictness, Roberts writes (1970: 49–50):

> Multiplication of copies by dictation was not allowed; each scroll had to be copied directly from another scroll; official copies, until A.D. 70 derived ultimately from a master copy in the Temple, were kept at first in a cupboard in each synagogue, later in a room adjoining it. The cupboard faced towards Jerusalem, and the rolls within it were the most holy objects of the synagogue.

There is ample evidence to show that several of the earliest New Testament manuscripts were manually copied from one manuscript to another (as opposed to copying by multiple dictation) and that Christians gave the same care to making accurate copies as did the Jews.

Furthermore, many of the early manuscripts display marginal notes, reading aids (accents, breathing marks, punctuation), and corrections, which, as Roberts indicates (1979: 22), may be a legacy from Judaism. Several of the papyri show the hand of a corrector (διορθωτής, *diorthōtēs*), for example, $\mathfrak{P}$5, $\mathfrak{P}$13, $\mathfrak{P}$15, $\mathfrak{P}$27, $\mathfrak{P}$46, $\mathfrak{P}$51, $\mathfrak{P}$66, $\mathfrak{P}$69, $\mathfrak{P}$75, and $\mathfrak{P}$91. And it is remarkable that three papyri ($\mathfrak{P}$13, $\mathfrak{P}$17, $\mathfrak{P}$46), all containing Hebrews, show the same kind of double punctuation marks to indicate the metrical flow of the text. Such markings could have originated with the writer of Hebrews himself and then been transmitted in successive copies.

Finally, it should be pointed out that many of the New Testament books were specifically written to be read in the church. This would put the New Testament writings on the same level as the Old Testament text, which was read aloud in the synagogue (Acts 13:27; 15:21) and in Christian assemblies (1 Cor. 14:26; Col. 3:16). The Greek word for "reading" meant to read aloud in public; and the Greek word for "reader" was used for the one who read the Scriptures aloud in the services of the synagogue (Luke 4:16) and in the Christian church (Col. 4:16; 1 Thess. 5:27).

The reader of the New Testament text to Christian churches is probably referred to in Matthew 24:15 and Mark 13:14 by way of a parenthetical expression: "Let the reader understand." Other passages clearly point to the one who read the Scriptures out loud to an assembly of believers. In 1 Timothy 4:13, Paul urged Timothy to "devote [himself] to the public reading of Scripture." Revelation 1:3 promises a blessing to "the one who reads the words of this prophecy"—speaking specifically of each of the readers who would read the Book of Revelation to each of the seven churches addressed in the book. And, finally, Paul admonished the believers to read his message so as to understand his knowledge in the mystery of Christ (Eph. 3:3–6). This is an exhortation to take his epistle—an encyclical to several churches—and read it out loud in public. This very act would validate the sacredness of the text.

Many of the New Testament books were originally produced as works of literature. For example, the four Gospels, Acts, Romans, Ephesians, Hebrews, 1 Peter, and Revelation were clearly designed from the beginning to be literary works reaching a large audience. Most of the other New Testament books are "occasional" letters, that is, letters written primarily to meet the need of the occasion.

Because they lived in a Hellenized world, the New Testament writers spoke, read, and wrote Greek—the common (koinē) language of the Greco-Roman world. Many of the New Testament writers knew other works of Greek literature and cited them. John alludes to Philo. Paul quotes the Cretan poet Epimenides (Acts 17:28: "In him we live and move and have our being"; and Titus 1:12: "Cretans are always liars, evil

brutes, lazy gluttons"—both from *Cretica*), the Cicilian poet
Aratus (Acts 17:28: "We are his offspring"—from *Phaenomena*),
and the Greek poet Menander (1 Cor. 15:32: "Let us eat and
drink, / for tomorrow we die"—from the Greek comedy *Thais*).
Paul's epistolary style is modeled after that first created by
Greek writers such as Isocrates and Plato. The Gospel writers
were typical Greek historiographers. Their works follow the
pattern set by the Greek historian Herodotus, who set a high
standard of observation and reporting.

These men had respect for books; they knew how to craft a
book and get it published. As was customary in those days, a
writer would often use an amanuensis. Tertius was Paul's
amanuensis for Romans (Rom. 16:23), and Silvanus was Peter's
amanuensis for 1 Peter (1 Pet. 5:12). Because Paul made special
mention in several epistles of writing the greeting in his own
hand (see Gal. 6:11; 2 Thess. 3:17; Col. 4:18), it is clear that he
used other amanuenses, who are not identified. Luke's two-
book work (Luke and Acts) was very likely sponsored (i.e.,
funded) by Theophilus (to whom Luke dedicated the books) and
published in multiple copies. As recorded by Eusebius (*Ecclesiastical History* 3:24:5–7), Irenaeus tells us that Mark and Luke
"published their Gospels"—using the Greek word ἐκδόσις, the
standard term for the public dissemination of any writing. Irenaeus (*Against Heresies* 3:1:1) also said, "John, the disciple of
the Lord, he who had leaned on his breast, also published
[ἐκδôκε] the Gospel, while living at Ephesus in Asia." For John
to "publish" his Gospel means that he (with the help of the
Johannine community) made a distribution of multiple copies
of his Gospel.

Paul wrote a few personal letters (to Timothy, Titus, and
Philemon) and several epistles. There is a difference between a
letter and an epistle. According to Adolf Deissmann (1927:
227–45), a letter is direct personal correspondence between two
people not intended to be read by others, whereas an epistle is a
stylized literary form that gives the impression of being per-
sonally directed to one or more individuals but whose real
intent is to address a much wider audience. Such was the intent
of many of Paul's epistles. For example, Paul instructed the
Colossians and Laodiceans to exchange epistles and read the
one sent to the neighboring church (Col. 4:16).

Two of Paul's epistles, Romans and Ephesians, were clearly intended, from their inception, to be encyclical treatises—read by all the churches. Of Paul's epistles, only three (excluding the pastorals) were written exclusively by Paul—without mentioning another coauthor per se, such as Timothy or Silas; the three are Romans, Galatians, and Ephesians. Galatians had to be authored only by Paul because it involves a personal defense; Romans and Ephesians are single-authored because each is a magnum opus. Romans is Paul's masterpiece on the Christian life, and Ephesians is Paul's masterpiece on the church. Those who have studied these works are convinced that Paul was a master of the Greek epistolary style. Paul probably kept copies of most of his epistles, especially his treatises. When Paul was in prison, he asked Timothy to bring "my scrolls, especially the parchments" (2 Tim. 4:13). The scrolls probably contained portions of the Septuagint, and the parchments (μεμβράνας, a loanword from Latin meaning "membrane") may have contained copies of various epistles Paul had previously written in the form of parchment codexes (see pp. 48–50 below).

The Book of Hebrews is also a literary masterpiece, perhaps written by Apollos, an Alexandrian Jew, familiar with Alexandrian allegorical hermeneutic. And the Book of Revelation, with its kaleidoscopic, symbolic, and apocalyptic presentation, is one of the most literary books in the Bible (Ryken 1992: 143–46).

The first readers of these works, whether Jewish Christians or Gentile Christians, would have been aware of both the spiritual and literary value of these texts. As such, some of those who were the first to make copies of these books would have done so with great respect for preserving the original text.

Many of the early copies of various books of the New Testament were copied by scribes who must have been aware that they were copying a sacred text—originally composed by their founding apostles, such as Peter, Matthew, John, and Paul. Certain books were treated as sacred from the onset—the four Gospels, Acts, the Pauline Epistles, and 1 Peter—while other books, which took a longer time to be "canonized," were perhaps treated with less textual fidelity—books such as 2 Peter and Jude, the pastoral Epistles, James, and Revelation. Canonization was perceived before it was pronounced—for some books, as early as the first century. For example, the Pauline corpus was formed as early as 75 and recognized as apostolic, authoritative literature. The writer of 2 Peter went so far as to categorize Paul's epistles along with "the other Scriptures" (2 Pet. 3:15–16). The four Gospels were also recognized as being authoritative as early as the second century.

Irenaeus in his work *Against Heresies* (written ca. 175) affirms the authoritative value of the four Gospels, Acts, the Pauline Epistles, some of the general Epistles, and Revelation. The Muratorion Canon (170–220), perhaps written by Hippolytus, affirms nearly the same books. And several early third-century fathers, such as Tertullian, Clement of Alexandria, and Origen, treated several of the New Testament books as worthy of being sacred Scripture. Once the entire New Testament canon was set (in 367 for the Eastern church [viz., the Thirty-ninth Paschal Letter of Athanasius] and in 397 for the Western church [viz., a conciliar decision at Carthage]), all twenty-seven books now in our Bible were treated as inspired Scripture. But prior to the formal canonization, various books had already been given that status informally and were treated as such by the scribes who copied them.

The early papyri show that nearly all the early Christians who made copies of the text used special abbreviations to designate divine titles (*nomina sacra*). The first divine names to be abbreviated were Ἰησοῦς (Jesus), written as $\overline{\text{IC}}$, with a suprascript line over the abbreviation, and κύριος (Lord), written as $\overline{\text{KC}}$—perhaps first used in Septuagint, where the divine name YHWH was translated as κύριος. Two other divine names were also abbreviated: Χριστός (Christ) as $\overline{\text{XC}}$ and θεός (God) as $\overline{\text{ΘC}}$. Two other words were also written as *nomina sacra*: πνεῦμα (Spirit) as $\overline{\text{ΠNA}}$ and πατήρ (Father) as $\overline{\text{ΠHP}}$. Though the creation of the *nomina sacra* may reflect the Jewish influence of the tetragrammaton (YHWH, the consonantal structure of the name Yahweh), abbreviating the divine names is an entirely new creation found exclusively in Christian documents. According to C. H. Roberts (1979: 45–46), the creation of this kind of writing system "presupposes a degree of control and organization. . . . The establishment of the practice would not have been left to the whims of a single community, still less to that of an individual scribe. . . . The system was too complex for the ordinary scribe to operate without rules or an authoritative exemplar."

Roberts believes that the system of *nomina sacra* was either developed by the church in Jerusalem before 70 or by the church in Antioch in the same time period or shortly thereafter. Historically, the church in Jerusalem, with its Jewish orientation, is known to have been enthralled with the name of Jesus—as a surrogate for the divine name Yahweh. Furthermore, it is very likely that the Christian gospel was first taken to Alexandria by Jewish Christians from Palestine. This would help explain why the *nomina sacra* appear in nearly all the early papyri discovered in Egypt. The formation of the *nomina sacra* could have just as easily been created in Antioch, which had become the center of Christianity for the Greek-speaking population (Roberts and Skeat 1987: 60–61).

No matter where the system of abbreviating the *nomina sacra* originated, it is evident that it was instituted by the primitive church community and followed by all Christians thereafter. The *nomina sacra* "belong to the oldest stratum of the Christian faith and may well be contemporary with the first authorized or authoritative Christian writing" (Roberts 1979: 46). It is quite possible that some of the New Testament writers themselves, for example, John (who wrote in the late first century), used the special abbreviations for the *nomina sacra*, which were then copied in successive manuscripts.

The universal presence of the *nomina sacra* in early Christian documents speaks loudly against the notion that the early period of textual transmission was characteristically "free." Christian scribes were following an established pattern, an "authorized" exemplar. As Roberts (1970: 64) says, "The remarkably uniform system of *nomina sacra* . . . suggests that at an early date there were standard copies of the Christian scriptures."

Accompanying the use of abbreviated *nomina sacra* in Christian documents is the phenomenon of the use of the codex by all the early Christians. Prior to the middle of the first century, all the Scriptures and other writings were written on scrolls. For example, Jesus read from a scroll when he delivered his address from Isaiah 61 in the Nazarene synagogue (Luke

4:17–20). Jews and non-Jews used scrolls; everyone in the Greco-Roman world used scrolls.

Then the codex (a book formed by folding pages and stitching them at the spine) appeared—probably first modeled after parchment notebooks. According to Roberts's hypothesis, John Mark, while living in Rome, used such a parchment notebook to record the sayings of Jesus (via Peter's preaching). The entire Gospel of Mark, then, was first published as a codex.[1] "A gospel once circulating in this format determined, partly by way of authority, partly by way of sentiment and symbol, that the proper form for the Christian scriptures was a codex, not a roll" (Turner 1968: 11). Thereafter, all portions of the New Testament were written on codexes. The codex was unique to Christianity until the end of the second century. Kenyon (1951: 110) writes, "Among all the papyri discovered in Egypt which can be assigned to the second century . . . no single pagan [i.e., non-Christian] manuscript . . . is in codex form." This practice (which began either in Rome or Antioch) was a clear break with Judaism and, again, shows a kind of uniformity in the formation and dissemination of the early text. The codex form enabled Christians to place several books together in one volume, which was an impossibility with respect to the scroll; for example, the Pauline Epistles (as in 𝔓46 and probably 𝔓15/16), two or more Gospels (as in 𝔓4/64/67, which had Matthew and Luke, and 𝔓75, which had Luke and John), or the Gospels and Acts (as in 𝔓45).

The New Testament may contain a reference (2 Tim. 4:13) to both scrolls and codexes—the former containing Old Testament writings; the latter, New Testament writings. It is not insignificant that Paul differentiated between two types of writing materials when he requested Timothy to bring to him in prison τὰ βιβλία, μάλιστα τὰς μεμβράνας (the scrolls, especially the parchments). The scrolls (probably made of papyrus) were unquestionably portions of the Old Testament (whether in

1. The codex form of the Gospel of Mark could account for the early loss of the last portion of Mark (filled in later by 16:9–20) inasmuch as it would not be difficult for the last leaf of a codex to become separated from the rest of the text. If Mark was originally written on a scroll, the last portion would have been kept intact, rolled inside the rest of the manuscript. See Roberts and Skeat 1987: 54–61.

Greek or Hebrew). The parchments were very likely parchment notebooks or codexes. J. N. D. Kelly (1963: 216) explains how the Greek word μεμβράνα (borrowed from the Latin term *membrana*) "was a technical term, from the first century B.C., for a codex, or leaf-book, made of parchment. Such codices were widely used for note-books, account-books, memoranda, first drafts of literary works, and other writings not meant for the public; it is also likely that they were being used for literary purposes in the first century A.D." These parchment codexes, a distinct form for New Testament writings, could have very likely contained copies of Paul's epistles.

Contrary to the common notion that many of the early New Testament papyri were produced by untrained scribes making personal copies of poor quality, several of the early New Testament papyri were produced with extreme care by educated and professional scribes. Paleographers have classified handwriting styles from the third century B.C. to the fourth century A.D. (and beyond). Many of the early New Testament papyri were written in what is called "the reformed documentary hand" (i.e., the scribe knew he was working on a manuscript that was not just a legal document but a literary work). In *The Birth of the Codex*, Roberts and Skeat (1987: 46) write:

> The Christian manuscripts of the second century, although not reaching a high standard of calligraphy, generally exhibit a competent style of writing which has been called "reformed documentary" and which is likely to be the work of experienced scribes, whether Christian or not. . . . And it is therefore a reasonable assumption that the scribes of the Christian texts received pay for their work.

Of course, not all the early New Testament manuscripts were produced by professionals, because the conscience of some would not have allowed them to receive pay for this sacred task. Philo (*On the Special Laws* 4:163) declared that the Scriptures should not be copied for money, but by students of the law. But this would not prohibit a Christian professional scribe from copying the Scriptures, nor would it deter a Christian community from seeking the services of a professional scribe.

In the opinion of paleographers, several early Christian writings have a professional look. Roberts (1979: 23) specifies the following: the late second-century Papyrus Oxyrhynchus 405 (containing a very early copy of Irenaeus's *Against Heresies*, which was written ca. 175–180) and the New Testament papyri 𝔓4/64/67 and 𝔓77. Concerning 𝔓4/64/67, which may have originated from Caesarea (see chap. 6), Roberts indicates that the text was divided into sections according to a system also found in 𝔓75 and in the great fourth-century manuscripts ℵ and B; this system clearly was not created by the scribe. Furthermore, this manuscript, written in handsome script, displays three different positions for punctuation, as well as omission and quotation signs (in a system similar to that found in 𝔓66). 𝔓4/64/67 was a thoroughgoing literary production and, therefore, Roberts (1979: 23) remarks, "Once again we find in a manuscript of this early period a characteristic that appears to be not specifically Egyptian but of wider application." 𝔓77, also a literary production written in an elegant hand, has "what was or became a standard system of chapter [i.e., paragraph] division as well as punctuation and breathing [marks]" (Roberts 1979: 23).

Several other early New Testament manuscripts look quite professional: 𝔓1, 𝔓5, 𝔓38, 𝔓39, 𝔓46, 𝔓66, and 𝔓75. These were written with uniform lettering throughout in what paleographers call "biblical uncial" or "biblical majuscule" (so named because the manuscripts were written in all capital [majuscule] Greek letters in a style characteristic of biblical texts). The styles differ from century to century, which helps paleographers determine dates for the various manuscripts. Some of the early papyri were written in a first-century biblical majuscule style (𝔓46), some in a second-century style (𝔓66), and some in third-to fourth-century style (𝔓47). The paleographic evidence reveals that several of the early manuscripts were copied carefully with precision and acumen—undoubtedly affected by Alexandrian scriptoral practices.

Soon after the gospel went to Alexandria, the Christians in that city began a catechetical school called the Didaskelion. No doubt, this school was influenced by the library in Alexandria (with its scriptorium) in the making of literary texts. At first, the Christians were occupied with the Old Testament text. The Jews in Alexandria had produced the Septuagint for this great library. The Christians adopted this text as their own and used it to prove the veracity of Jesus' claim as Messiah. Christian exposition of the Septuagint caused the Jews to abandon it and make new translations of the Hebrew text. But Christians in the Alexandrian church continued to use the Septuagint as the basis of their apologetics and exposition. At the same time, they also used various New Testament books for instruction and exposition.

The church in Alexandria in the beginning was very likely composed of Jewish Christians drawn from Alexandria's large Jewish population. Many historians believe that the early church in Alexandria had its closest ties with Jewish Christians from Jerusalem and Palestine. This connection would have had an impact on the way the early Christians treated the Scriptures.

Coupled with this Jewish heritage would be the Alexandrian scriptoral heritage. Both would make Alexandria the prime city in all of Christendom to preserve the original text. By the end of the second century we know that Clement of Alexandria had commented on almost every book of the New Testament. Since he had learned at the feet of Pantaenus, we can safely assume that Pantaenus also used the New Testament literature. And Origen, who learned from both Pantaenus and Clement, provided commentaries on entire New Testament books—such as Matthew and John. Textual scholars have determined that the New Testament text used by Clement of Alexandria and Origen aligns with those Alexandrian manuscripts that are considered the best witnesses to the text. Thus, we can assume that Pantaenus and his predecessors must have also used a text that greatly resembled the original text.

Scriptoral practices in rural Egypt (i.e., the Fayum, Oxyrhynchus, etc.) beginning in the second century were influenced by the work of the professional scribes working in the scriptorium for the great library at Alexandria or perhaps by a Christian scriptorium founded in Alexandria (in association with the catechetical school) in the second century. Eusebius (*Ecclesiastical History* 5:10:1) implies that the school began well before the time Pantaenus was in charge of it (160–180). And Zuntz (1953: 279) quite convincingly argues that the Pauline corpus was produced using at least methods of Alexandrian scholarship—or maybe even in Alexandria itself—at the beginning of the second century (ca. 100). Functioning as the most ancient of the New Testament textual critics, the Alexandrian scribes selected the best manuscripts and then produced a text that reflected what they considered to be the original text. They must have worked with manuscripts having the same quality as 𝔓1, 𝔓4/64/67, 𝔓27, 𝔓46, 𝔓75, 𝔓77, etc.

Zuntz also argues (1953: 273) that by the middle of the second century the Alexandrian bishopric possessed a scriptorium, which by its output set the standard for the Alexandrian type of biblical manuscript. This standard could have included the codification of *nomina sacra,* the use of codexes, and other literary features. However, saying that Alexandria set a standard does not necessarily mean that Alexandria was exerting a kind of textual uniformity throughout Egypt during the second and early third centuries. It was not until the fourth century, when Athanasius became bishop of Alexandria, that Alexandria began to exert control over the Egyptian churches. This may have extended to the production of New Testaments, but certainly would not have reached every church. Prior to the third century, the manuscripts do not give evidence of having been produced at a central scriptorium. Rather, each manuscript was produced by a scriptorium associated with a local church. Nevertheless, it is quite evident that a scriptoral standard had been set by Alexandria and that certain major Egyptian cities (such as Oxyrhynchus) were influenced by this standard.

Alexandrian scriptoral practices had become influential throughout the entire Hellenized world by the time the church first began. As early as the third century B.C. the Alexandrian library had over half-a-million volumes and had become a center of learning—like a modern university. Kenyon (1951: 27) elaborates:

> Besides being a library, it was an Academy of Letters and Learning. Eminent men of letters and scholars, such as Callimachus, Apollonius Rhodius, and Aristarchus, were placed in succession at its head; students gathered round it; a corps of copyists was employed to multiply manuscripts; and Alexandria became the centre of the literary life of the Hellenistic world.

Once Rome awoke to an intellectual life, it absorbed Alexandrian learning and books. Throughout the Greco-Roman world, libraries were patterned after Alexandria's. Pergamus, with its library of two hundred thousand volumes, was situated near Ephesus in the heart of Asia Minor—the site of the earliest churches founded by Paul and ministered to by John. The library in Rome (burnt by Nero) was restored by Domitian and refurbished with copies from Alexandria. And there was also a library in Antioch, accompanied by a university. Thus, four of the great centers of learning in the Greco-Roman world were also four of the most important centers for the early church: Alexandria, Rome, Pergamus, and Antioch. The churches in these cities could not help but be affected by these centers of learning and publishing—especially with respect to the making of books.

The scriptoral practices in these libraries would have followed Alexandrian philological traditions. Furthermore, there would have been a spillover effect into the general bookmaking trade. Among those who used and read books there would have been some who had developed an appreciation for preserving the original text. And among these would have been some Christians who were thoroughly Hellenized and educated in the practice of making faithful copies of a literary text. Even if some Christians did not consciously appreciate the notion of preserving the original wording from a theological perspective, there would have been others who, from a philological perspective, would have been concerned about copying the original wording. According to Zuntz (1953: 270–83), such people were not hard to find among Christians living in a Hellenized world, wherein Alexandrian practices were pervasive.

The very first copies of various books of the New Testament should have been produced with accuracy because they were the archetypal copies for the author himself and for the original recipient (usually a particular local church). The earliest copies could have been made by the author himself, his amanuensis, or a coworker. The recipients who made copies would have been careful to preserve the original wording because a living author could verify the accuracy. Although this respect for the original wording could have become more lax after the death of the apostles, there must have been some who were intent on preserving the original wording of the apostolic teachings.

Since all the Gospels were "published" (see pp. 44–46 above) and distributed in multiple copies so as to be read in various churches, the very first copies were those made under the auspices of the authors. For example, Eusebius (*Ecclesiastical History* 2:15) said that the history of Jesus' ministry written by Mark was authorized by Peter to be read in the churches. It is quite likely that an author like Mark would have kept a copy of his own work and had another made for Peter. Luke definitely would have kept a copy of his Gospel—if only for the reason that he would need to refer to it in making the sequel, the Book of Acts. And the Johannine community (which included the Ephesian elders that encouraged John to write his Gospel) would have both dispatched copies and kept copies for themselves. The Revelation written by John also had to have been produced in multiple copies from the onset because it was addressed to seven local churches in Asia (Rev. 1:4). Each church would have received a copy of the Apocalypse.

Some of Paul's epistles give us a few hints about some of the very earliest copies. The exchange of epistles between the Colossians and Laodiceans (referred to in Col. 4:16) would have necessitated the making of copies. The encyclical epistle called Ephesians would have been multicopied from the onset—with the name of each local church filled in for each copy. Paul would have also kept a copy of this epistle, since it is a treatise on the church, as well as a copy of Romans, since it is a treatise on the plan of salvation. Paul also seems to have kept copies of the letters he wrote to the Corinthians (1 Cor. 5:9; 2 Cor. 2:4). Various churches would have kept copies of the epistle(s) sent directly to them and then, later, requested copies of epistles initially sent to neighboring churches.

After Paul's death, it would have been natural for someone or some church to collect his epistles into one corpus. There are two likely candidates: Timothy or Luke.

Prior to his death, Paul had charged Timothy to guard the sacred trust (deposit) and to commit the safekeeping of this trust to other faithful men (see 1 Tim. 6:20; 2 Tim. 1:12, 14; 2:2). This "deposit" (παραθήκη) refers to the apostolic teaching—in its oral form (explicitly) and in its written form (implicitly)—for how else could the sacred trust be passed on from generation to generation? Surely, Paul would have known that passing on the apostolic tradition would necessitate written documentation to accompany the oral tradition.

Another likely candidate would be Luke, a close companion of Paul and one very interested in passing on the apostolic traditions through his own writings. The Christian catechism (from κατηχέω—a technical term for Christian instruction, see 1 Cor. 14:19; Gal. 6:6), first given orally, would need written substantiation. Hence, Paul enscribed the apostolic proclamation in writing. Luke wrote his Gospel to substantiate what Theophilus had been taught orally through a kind of catechism (Luke 1:4). With the ending of the apostolic age (i.e., the time when there were no more living apostles), it became more and more important to have written documentation of the gospel and Christian truths. As the oral tradition was supposed to be safeguarded, so also the written tradition. Christians would have respected and wanted to preserve both.

The early New Testament papyri contribute virtually no new substantial variants, suggesting that all of the New Testament variants are preserved somewhere in the extant manuscript tradition. Kenyon (1958: 55) says:

> The number of manuscripts of the New Testament, of early translations from it, and of quotations from it in the oldest writers of the church, is so large that it is practically certain that the true reading of every doubtful passage is preserved in some one or other of these ancient authorities. This can be said of no other ancient book.

This tells us that it is very unlikely that we would find additional significant variant readings if other manuscripts were discovered—even if these manuscripts were from the first century. We can safely assume, then, that the original text has usually been preserved in the earliest manuscripts.

To summarize, the making of New Testament manuscripts was more of an ecclesiastical affair than a personal affair. Manuscripts were made to be read aloud in the church meetings. We know that in the days of the early church there was one designated as a "reader" (Greek, ἀναγνώστης; Latin, *lector*). His task was to read aloud the Scriptures to the congregation. H. Leitzmann says that these readers "understood the difficult art of reading aloud at public worship with melodic and rhythmic correctness the prescribed Biblical lessons out of codices written without word-division or punctuation" (cited in Turner 1977: 84–85). Several of the New Testament papyri were written in larger than usual type so as to facilitate oral reading in an assembly. This is true of the two Oxyrhynchus papyri, 𝔓1 and 𝔓5, as well as for the two Bodmer papyri, 𝔓66 and 𝔓75. Other Greek Old Testament manuscripts were also written in larger type to facilitate reading: Chester Beatty Papyri VIII–XII, containing Jeremiah, Esther, Daniel, Ezekiel, Ecclesiasticus, and Enoch, as well as the Yale Genesis (Turner 1977: 84–86).

Of course, some copies were made for personal use (such as 𝔓18, 𝔓72, 𝔓93), but most of the papyri were written for churches. We know this because they were written on large pages in a professional or documentary hand, exhibiting reading aids (such as punctuation, spaces for paragraphs, breathing marks) and corrections. Such papyri include 𝔓1, 𝔓4/64/67, 𝔓5, 𝔓13, 𝔓15/16, 𝔓17, 𝔓21, 𝔓23, 𝔓24, 𝔓27, 𝔓30, 𝔓32, 𝔓37, 𝔓38, 𝔓39, 𝔓46, 𝔓53, 𝔓65, 𝔓66, 𝔓69, 𝔓75, 𝔓77, 𝔓90, and 𝔓92. Copies of the biblical books would be kept in the place of worship and also in the houses of the readers themselves. See, for example, the story cited in chapter 1 (p. 15 above) about the mayor of Cirta and Bishop Paul. After only one copy of the Christian Scriptures was found, Paul told the mayor, "We haven't any more . . . the readers [lectors] have the books" (Stevenson 1957: 287–89). The point is that each church had several copies of the Scriptures. It is safe to assume that these copies would have been identical (or nearly so) for the sake of having a uniform text in the local assembly.

Some of the early manuscripts appear to have been produced in a scriptorium, for they bear the marks of several correctors. Unless they were produced in the Alexandria scriptorium and transported to the Fayum, these manuscripts bear record of scriptoria existing in rural Egypt. It is not unreasonable to presume that the scribes producing these copies would have wanted to make accurate copies for their congregation. The adjustments of the correctors in manuscripts such as 𝔓46 and 𝔓66 show that the manuscripts were, in fact, made more accurate.

Many of the early New Testament manuscripts that have been discovered were originally produced for churches. The Chester Beatty papyri and the Bodmer papyri are believed to have been part of a church or monastary library, as were several of the Oxyrhynchus papryi. As such, these manuscripts would have been produced with meticulousness and care.

By presenting these arguments, I do not pretend to be making a defense for the textual fidelity of *all* the early New Testament manuscripts. There are obviously some manuscripts that were poorly made. Many of these manuscripts were made by individuals for use or were made by scribes who exerted tremendous liberties. Furthermore, it is quite evident that several scribes altered the text due to the influence of the oral tradition or of what they had read in other Gospels (harmonization is a major textual phenomenon). And, finally, it must be admitted that some of the early scribes were more intent on transmitting the message of the text than the actual words of the text. This is clearly evidenced in manuscripts such as $\mathfrak{P}$45. Nonetheless, there are several extant manuscripts that display all the markings of textual fidelity. To these we must look in our quest to recover the original wording of the Greek New Testament.

Chapter Five

MANUSCRIPTS BURIED IN SAND: THE OXYRHYNCHUS NEW TESTAMENT

I t would be wonderful if we could uncover the books of the ancient Alexandrian library. Unfortunately, this is a pipe dream because the Alexandrian library was destroyed twice over—and, even if the books had not been destroyed by fire, they would have been obliterated by moisture. We have to look elsewhere for our ancient manuscripts—within the interior of Egypt, to those cities that had ancient Christian communities and whose climate could preserve ancient texts.

Our quest for the original text of the Greek New Testament first takes us to Oxyrhynchus, Egypt, a city that had many significant connections with Alexandria (especially with regard to scholarship). According to E. G. Turner (1956), there were a number of Alexandrians who owned property in Oxyrhynchus, several of whom were professors at the famous Alexandrian museum. Some of these professors, while living in Oxyrhynchus, corresponded with certain Alexandrians about obtaining copies of various works of literature. These copies would have been produced by the Alexandrian scriptorium and then sent to Oxyrhynchus. In other words, certain manuscripts found in Oxyrhynchus would have been produced in Alexandria.

Oxyrhynchus also had its own scriptorium that was responsible for the production of literary works. It is safe to assume the existence of a scriptorium because the literary papyri discovered in Oxyrhynchus show that a limited number of scribes were engaged in writing the texts of Greek literature. Turner (1956) has been able to identify ten specific scribes in Oxyrhynchus who worked on making copies of literary texts in the second century. It is possible that some Christian manuscripts were also produced by these scribes or in the same scriptorium (or even in a separate scriptorium serving the church in Oxyrhynchus). It appears that some of the same scribes worked on two or more religious documents. For example, the same scribe produced $\mathfrak{P}$20 and $\mathfrak{P}$27; another scribe produced both $\mathfrak{P}$22 and Papyrus Oxyrhynchus 546 (the Gospel according to Thomas); another produced $\mathfrak{P}$90 and Papyrus Oxyrhynchus 656 (Genesis); and yet another scribe made both $\mathfrak{P}$17 and Papyrus Oxyrhynchus 850 (the Acts of John).

Roberts believes that Oxyrhynchus was probably an intellectual center for Christianity in rural Egypt. This is suggested by the presence of an autograph manuscript of an anti-Jewish dialogue (Papyrus Oxyrhynchus 2070), dated in the third century, and by the number of Christian manuscripts discovered in Oxyrhynchus. For every one manuscript extant, there must be at least a hundred (if not more) that did not survive. And, usually, every extant manuscript preserves only a portion of the entire original document. Thus, Roberts (1979: 24) affirms the existence of a Christian scriptorium in Oxyrhynchus as early as the late second century.

Of all the manuscripts discovered in Oxyrhynchus many are nonliterary documents (i.e., letters, legal documents, business transactions); they were written by common folk—"tradesmen, farmers, minor government officials to whom knowledge of and writing in Greek was an essential skill, but who had few or no literary interests" (Roberts 1979: 21). Other manuscripts were literary—such as the works of Homer, Pindar, Philo, and books of the Bible. Copies of these literary works were often produced by professionals or by those acquainted with professional scriptoral practices. Of the early Christian manuscripts, Roberts and Skeat (1987: 46) say:

The Christian manuscripts of the second century, although not reaching a high standard of calligraphy, generally exhibit a competent style of writing which has been called "reformed documentary" and which is likely to be the work of experienced scribes, whether Christian or not.

Among these writers were Christians who must have lived in Oxyrhynchus as early as the middle of the second century, if not earlier. We know this because there are several early biblical manuscripts, both of the Greek Old Testament and the Greek New Testament, which date as early as the second century and therefore give testimony to a Christian community existing in the same period. There are several other significant Christian documents from Oxyrhynchus that date to the second and third centuries: Papyrus Oxyrhynchus 405, the late second-century fragment mentioned above that contains part of Irenaeus's *Against Heresies*; Papyrus Oxyrhynchus 1786, a fragment of a Christian hymn praising the Trinity (dated to the third century); and Papyrus Oxyrhynchus 3025, an order by the president of the council of Oxyrhynchus (dated Feb. 28, 256) to arrest a certain Petosarapis, who is called a "Christian" (Χριστιανός)—the earliest instance of this title in the Oxyrhynchus papyri.

By the end of the third century we know that there were a few Christian churches in Oxyrhynchus. There is explicit evidence of a church existing in Oxyrhynchus as early as 303. Bishop Peter of Alexandria fled there in 303 and discovered that Oxyrhynchus had a bishop and a core of enthusiasts called φιλοπόνοι (literally "lovers of labor"—laborious, industrious men) who assisted the clergy to hold together the community of believers. (It is not unreasonable to imagine that Bishop Peter brought with him New Testament manuscripts from Alexandria to Oxyrhynchus so as to keep them from being confiscated.) In the fourth century, Christianity blossomed in Oxyrhynchus, and by its end there were at least thirty churches in Oxyrhynchus (Schmidt 1901: 6–7; Turner 1968: 150).

In 1897 Grenfell and Hunt went to Oxyrhynchus (now called al-Bahnasa or Behnesa) because they knew that the Christian church had become established in Oxyrhynchus both before and after the Diocletian persecution (ca. 303), and it was supposed that the citizens would be able to afford libraries of literary texts. Concerning their choice of Oxyrhynchus, Grenfell (1897: 1) writes:

> Being the capital of the Nome, it must have been the abode of many rich persons who could afford to possess a library of literary texts. Though the ruins of the old town were known to be fairly extensive, and it was probable that most of them were of the Graeco-Roman period, neither town nor cemetery appeared to have been plundered for antiquities in recent times. Above all, Oxyrhynchus seemed to be a site where fragments of Christian literature might be expected of an earlier date than the fourth century, to which our oldest manuscripts of the New Testament belong; for the place was renowned in the fourth and fifth centuries on account of the number of its churches and monasteries.

When Grenfell and Hunt went to Oxyrhynchus, they did not find papyri in ancient cemeteries, tombs, churches, or monasteries—places excavators usually looked. Rather, they found them in ancient rubbish heaps. Manuscripts found in rubbish heaps are not "rubbish" per se or defective copies. When a manuscript became old and worn, it was customary to replace it with a fresh copy and discard the old one. Since the Egyptians are known to have disposed of such copies by putting them into rubbish heaps, excavators looking for ancient Egyptian papyri would search for ancient rubbish heaps in deserted sites on ground higher than the Nile River. Grenfell and Hunt's choice of the ancient rubbish heap at Oxyrhynchus was fortuitous, for it yielded that largest cache of papyri ever discovered.

On the second day of the dig (in 1897), Grenfell and Hunt unearthed the "Sayings of Jesus" or "Logia" (later identified as part of the Gospel according to Thomas) and a papyrus leaf, now known as $\mathfrak{P}$1, containing Matthew 1:1–18 (on the recto and verso). In 1898 the first volume of *The Oxyrhynchus Papyri* was published and it included these two texts. The discovery of $\mathfrak{P}$1 proved to be a promising beginning of many more discoveries.

Grenfell and Hunt continued to go to Oxyrhynchus several years thereafter in search of ancient papyri. The fifth season was extremely fortuitous because they discovered the literary remains of two scholars' libraries. In 1905 the first literary remains were uncovered (Grenfell and Hunt 1906: 10):

> On January 13 and 14 we were fortunate enough to make incomparably the largest and most important find of classical pieces that we have ever made. . . . Shortly before sunset [on January 13] we reached, at about 6 feet from the surface, a place where in the third century A.D. a basketful of broken literary papyrus rolls had been thrown away. . . . Before being condemned to the rubbish heap, the papyri had as usual been torn up.

Among the classical works discovered in this basketful of papyri were pieces of unknown classical works: an extensive manuscript of Pindar's *Paeans*, a history of the fourth century B.C. written by Cratippus, "the Oxyrhynchus Historian" (so called by Grenfell and Hunt), Plato's *Symposium*, and the *Panegyricus* of Isocrates.

Near the end of the season they discovered the literary remains of another scholar who was quite interested in the writings of the lyric poets. Grenfell and Hunt (1906: 12) describe the find as follows:

> The remainder of the season was practically devoted to clearing another large and high mound in which we were fortunate enough to discover the remains of a second classical library within a few days after we had begun work on it. . . . The evidence of the documents found below the literary texts shows that the latter must have been thrown away in the fifth century; but the MSS. themselves are chiefly of the second and third century. Compared with the first find, the second is in point of bulk more than twice as large, and the MSS. probably exceed thirty in number; but as a whole it is hardly likely to prove so valuable, since the papyri have been much more broken up.

Among the manuscripts found in this lot were a hexameter hymn to Hermes, a fragment of a lost comedy by Menander, fragments of Sophocles' *Antigone*, Euripides' *Hecuba*, and the *Argonautica* of Appolonius Rhodius.

Among the classical works of both libraries were found several New Testament fragments. According to what Grenfell and Hunt wrote in the forewords to volumes 5–13 of *The Oxyrhynchus Papyri* concerning the provenance of the manuscripts published in these volumes, it can be ascertained that 𝔓15/16, 𝔓28, 𝔓29, and 𝔓30 came from the first library and that 𝔓17, 𝔓18, 𝔓20, 𝔓21, 𝔓22, 𝔓23, 𝔓24, and 𝔓27 came from the second library. The presence of these fragments (each representing a full New Testament book) among classical works suggests the literary worth of these biblical manuscripts.

Grenfell and Hunt excavated at Oxyrhynchus until 1907; the Italian exploration society (under G. Vitelli) continued the work there during the years 1910–13 and 1927–34.

In total, thirty-six papyrus manuscripts containing portions of the New Testament have been discovered at Oxyrhynchus. Almost all of these are dated between 200 and 400, and a few have been dated to the second century: 𝔓32 (ca. 175), 𝔓52 (115–125), 𝔓77 (ca. 150), and 𝔓90 (ca. 175). A few other papyri have been dated to the end of the second century (ca. 200): 𝔓1, 𝔓13, and 𝔓27. (In his 1988 article arguing that 𝔓46 [not from Oxyrhynchus] should be dated around 80, Kim also suggests early dates for some Oxyrhynchus papyri as well; see pp. 30–31 above.) By 1922 twenty-one of these papyri were published in *The Oxyrhynchus Papyri*: 𝔓1, 𝔓5, 𝔓9, 𝔓10, 𝔓13, 𝔓15, 𝔓16, 𝔓17, 𝔓18, 𝔓19, 𝔓20, 𝔓21, 𝔓22, 𝔓23, 𝔓24, 𝔓26, 𝔓27, 𝔓28, 𝔓29, 𝔓30, and 𝔓39. One papyrus was published in the same series in 1941 (𝔓51), three more in 1957 (𝔓69, 𝔓70, and 𝔓71), two in 1968 (𝔓77 and 𝔓78), and one in 1983 (𝔓90). Three additional Oxyrhynchus New Testament papyri were published in *Papiri Greci e Latini della Societa Italiana*: 𝔓35, 𝔓36, and 𝔓48. A few other papyri are thought to have come from Oxyrhynchus: 𝔓32 (Hunt 1911: 10–11), 𝔓52 (Roberts 1935), 𝔓82 (Schwartz 1968) and 𝔓85 (Schwartz 1969). And there is one Princeton Papyrus manuscript (P.15) that came from Oxyrhynchus: 𝔓54. In addition to the papyrus manuscripts, several vellum New Testament manuscripts were discovered at Oxyrhynchus. Those published in *The Oxyrhynchus Papyri* are 069, 071, 0162, 0163, 0169, and 0206. Three other vellum manuscripts from Oxyrhynchus were published in *Papiri Greci e Latini della Societa Italiana*: 0172, 0173, and 0176. (Through correspondence with Revell Coles, one of the current editors of the Oxyrhynchus papyri, I was told that there are many more papyri awaiting publication.)

Although most of the Oxyrhynchus manuscripts are quite fragmentary (usually containing only a few leaves or folios), they have provided a broad sampling of many verses from eighteen books in the New Testament. The following arrangement shows the coverage book by book through the New Testament:

Matthew

$\mathfrak{P}$1	1:1–9, 12, 14–20
$\mathfrak{P}$19	10:32–11:5
$\mathfrak{P}$21	12:24–26, 32–33
$\mathfrak{P}$35	25:12–15, 20–23
$\mathfrak{P}$70	2:13–16; 2:22–3:1; 11:26–27; 12:4–5; 24:3–6, 12–15
$\mathfrak{P}$71	19:10–11, 17–18
$\mathfrak{P}$77	23:30–39
071	1:21–24; 1:25–2:2

Mark

069	10:50–51; 11:11–12

Luke

$\mathfrak{P}$69	22:41, 45–48, 58–61
$\mathfrak{P}$82	7:32–34, 37–38

John

$\mathfrak{P}$5	1:23–31, 33–40; 16:14–30; 20:11–17, 19–20, 22–25 (see appendix)
$\mathfrak{P}$22	15:25–16:2; 16:21–32
$\mathfrak{P}$28	6:8–12, 17–22
$\mathfrak{P}$36	3:14–18, 31–32, 34–35
$\mathfrak{P}$39	8:14–22
$\mathfrak{P}$52	18:31–33, 37–38
$\mathfrak{P}$90	18:36–19:7
0162	2:11–22

Acts

$\mathfrak{P}$29	26:7–8, 20
$\mathfrak{P}$48	23:11–17, 23–29

Romans

$\mathfrak{P}$10	1:1–7
$\mathfrak{P}$26	1:1–16
$\mathfrak{P}$27	8:12–22, 24–27; 8:33–9:3; 9:5–9
0172	1:27–30; 1:32–2:2

1 Corinthians

$\mathfrak{P}$15	7:18–8:4

Galatians

$\mathfrak{P}$51	1:2–10, 13, 16–20
0176	3:16–25

Philippians
𝔓16   3:10–17; 4:2–8

1 Thessalonians
𝔓30   4:12–13, 16–17; 5:3, 8–10, 12–18, 25–28

2 Thessalonians
𝔓30   1:1–2

Titus
𝔓32   1:11–15; 2:3–8

Hebrews
𝔓13   2:14–5:5; 10:8–22; 10:29–11:13; 11:28–12:17
𝔓17   9:12–19

James
𝔓20   2:19–3:9
𝔓23   1:10–12, 15–18
𝔓54   2:16–18, 22–26; 3:2–4
0173   1:25–27

1 Peter
0206   5:5–13

1 John
𝔓9   4:11–12, 14–17

Jude
𝔓78   4–5, 7–8

Revelation
𝔓18   1:4–7
𝔓24   5:5–8; 6:5–8
𝔓85   9:19–10:2; 10:5–9
0163   16:17–20
0169   3:19–4:3

In addition to the canonical books, the Oxyrhynchus papyri include the very popular Shepherd of Hermes (Oxyrhynchus Papyri 404, 1172, 1599, 1783, 3526, 3527, 3528), the Didache (1782), the Gospel according to Thomas (1, 654, 655), the Gospel of Peter (2949), some unidentified noncanonical gospels (840, 1224), the Acts of Paul (6, 1602), the Acts of Peter (849), the Acts of John (850), and the Gospel of Mary (3525).

Most of the New Testament manuscripts were made for use in churches, which means they were made to be read aloud. Manuscripts such as 𝔓1, 𝔓24, and 𝔓30 were part of church Bibles. Christians also made copies of the Septuagint, especially the Pentateuch and the Psalms,[1] also for the purpose of being read in church meetings. Other manuscripts were made for personal use (such as 𝔓10, which was an amulet or a schoolboy's exercise, and 0169, which came from a miniature codex of Revelation).

There is hardly any overlap of coverage among the New Testament manuscripts, which is unfortunate because it limits comparative study of a strictly local text. The few manuscripts that do have overlap are 𝔓5 and 𝔓22, and 𝔓52 and 𝔓90. The first pair is strikingly dissimilar. Grenfell and Hunt (1897–: 10.14–16) say that 𝔓22 is "a good and interesting text, but does not at all agree consistently with any one of the chief authorities." Following Grenfell and Hunt, Schofield (1936: 196–99) indicates that 𝔓22's "textual affinities are not strongly marked; it does not agree with any one group of the manuscripts. The fragment rather represents the eclecticism of the early papyri before the crystalizing of the textual families had taken place." In significant variation units, 𝔓22 rarely agrees with 𝔓5, which shows that two manuscripts can exist side by side in the same locality at the same time and yet contain significantly different texts. 𝔓52 and 𝔓90 exhibit less than ten words in common because 𝔓52 is such a small fragment; nonetheless, all the words are exactly the same (see K. Aland 1986).

Although little comparative study can be done among the Oxyrhynchus papyri, these manuscripts can be compared with other early Egyptian papyri. Several of the Oxyrhynchus papyri contain the same material as other early papyri discovered in the Fayum (a region near Oxyrhynchus—both of which are situated in Middle Egypt). Thus, it is possible to do a comparative textual study of a "regional" text (which is what most textual theorists would call a "local" text) in the broader sense. Quite

1. The following books of the Greek Old Testament have been recovered from Oxyrhynchus, each followed by the manuscript number in *The Oxyrhynchus Papyri*: Genesis (656, 1007, 1166, 1167), Exodus (1074, 1075), Leviticus (1225, 1351), Joshua (1168), Job (3522), Ecclesiastes (2066), Psalms (845, 1226, 1352, 1779, 2065), and Amos (846).

naturally, one would want to compare the Oxyrhynchus papyri with the Chester Beatty papyri (𝔓45, 𝔓46, 𝔓47) to see if there is any kind of great affinity or noticeable diversity among Egyptian manuscripts with similar dating (early second century to early fourth century). There are some striking affinities between a few Oxyrhynchus papyri and two of the Beatty manuscripts: 𝔓13 (the most substantial of the Oxyrhynchus papyri) has great affinity with 𝔓46 (seventy-one agreements and only seventeen disagreements; see Kenyon 1933–58: 3/sup. xv) and 𝔓85 is in accord with 𝔓47 (see Comfort 1990a: 66).

For the most part, the Oxyrhynchus New Testament (as I have called it) has a variegated textual character, with strong Alexandrian affinities. Most of the Gospel manuscripts show an affinity with the fourth-century manuscripts ℵ (namely, 𝔓5, 𝔓28, 𝔓77) and B (namely, 𝔓1, 𝔓39, 𝔓71); but some of them exhibit marked independence—such as 𝔓21, 𝔓22, 𝔓69, and 𝔓90. The two Acts papyri (𝔓29 and 𝔓48) display Western tendencies—which seems to uphold the view that one of the earliest forms of Acts was "Western" in textual character (Metzger 1971: 259–72). Among the manuscripts containing the Pauline Epistles, some show great affinity with ℵ (namely, 𝔓15/16 and 𝔓32), others with B (namely, 𝔓27). The manuscript containing a large portion of Hebrews, 𝔓13, greatly resembles 𝔓46, while 𝔓17, having a small portion of Hebrews, resembles later Byzantine texts. In the general Epistles, 𝔓20 agrees with B, and 𝔓23 with ℵ, B, and C (a trustworthy multiple witness to the Book of James), while 𝔓9 and 𝔓78 exhibit independence. 𝔓18 and 𝔓24 have strong affinity with the best multiple witness to the Book of Revelation (ℵ, A, and C), while 𝔓85 shows some agreement with 𝔓47 and ℵ. The complete Oxyrhynchus New Testament text shows a strong relationship with 𝔓66, 𝔓75, ℵ, and B in the Gospels (with some independence); with the "Western" text and D in Acts; with ℵ, B, and 𝔓46 in the Pauline Epistles; with ℵ, B, and C in the general Epistles (with some independence); and with ℵ, A, C, and 𝔓47 in Revelation.

One can hypothesize that manuscripts produced at Oxyrhynchus were of two kinds: those produced by nonprofessional scribes (quite often for personal use) and those produced by professional scribes or men educated in scriptoral practices (usually for church use). The nonprofessional manuscripts were usually written in a documentary hand, while the more professional manuscripts were written in a trained literary or reformed documentary hand. The professional manuscripts are reflective of Alexandrian scriptoral practices—or perhaps were even produced in Alexandria—while the nonprofessional manuscripts are reflective and typical of the kind of manuscripts that existed throughout all of Egypt and perhaps throughout the Mediterranean world. I say "typical" because the Egyptian churches were not unlike other churches in the second and third centuries, and Egyptian scribal practices (outside of Alexandria) were very much like other scribal practices in the Greco-Roman world (Roberts 1979: chap. 3; Skeat [in *Oxyrhynchus Papyri*, vol. 50 (1983), pp. 3–5], on the basis of $\mathfrak{P}$90, makes a good case for Roberts's thesis).

Among the more literary (or professionally made) New Testament manuscripts discovered at Oxyrhynchus are a few noteworthy documents: $\mathfrak{P}$1, $\mathfrak{P}$5, $\mathfrak{P}$13, $\mathfrak{P}$39, and $\mathfrak{P}$77. These manuscripts were written with uniform lettering throughout in what paleographers call "biblical uncial." $\mathfrak{P}$77, a second-century manuscript, is a thoroughgoing literary production written in an elegant hand, with paragraph divisions, punctuation, and breathing marks (Roberts 1979: 23). Furthermore, $\mathfrak{P}$77 greatly resembles the work of one particular scribe at Oxyrhynchus who produced copies of literary works: Papyrus Oxyrhynchus 1082 (Cercidas) and Papyrus Oxyrhynchus 1247 (Thucydides) (see the editors' comments on Papyrus Oxyrhynchus 2683 [$\mathfrak{P}$77] and Turner 1956: 146 [esp. scribe 4]). In $\mathfrak{P}$13, also an excellent literary production, the text of Hebrews was written on the back of a papyrus containing the new epitome of Livy. Therefore, it is likely that this manuscript was brought to Egypt by a Roman official and left behind when he left his post. (An auxiliary Roman cohort was stationed in Oxyrhynchus as early as the second century A.D.) Since $\mathfrak{P}$13 is so closely linked with $\mathfrak{P}$46, we can surmise that $\mathfrak{P}$13 was likely copied from a manuscript that originated in Alexandria (see full discussion in chap. 6).

These kinds of manuscripts are those that best represent the original text of the New Testament and were typical of the kinds of manuscripts the Alexandrians sought when making exemplars and archetypes for future copying.

In conclusion, one final question remains: was the Greek New Testament read by the Oxyrhynchian Christians different from the one commonly read today (i.e., Nestle–Aland's 26th edition of *Novum Testamentum Graece* and the United Bible

Societies' third edition of *The Greek New Testament*) or were there significant differences?

The early Oxyrhynchus manuscripts are cited about 150 times in the apparatus of NA[26]—about 90 times in support of the text and about 60 times for variant readings. This means that the Oxyrhynchus New Testament agrees with NA[26] 60% of the time and disagrees 40%. Of the readings that support the text, the Oxyrhynchus papyri were, in a few instances, instrumental in providing support for a change in the Nestle text (from the twenty-fifth edition to the twenty-sixth). Some noteworthy passages are as follows: Matthew 23:38 ($\mathfrak{P}$77); Romans 8:34 ($\mathfrak{P}$27 with $\mathfrak{P}$46); Hebrews 3:6 ($\mathfrak{P}$13 and $\mathfrak{P}$46); Hebrews 4:2 ($\mathfrak{P}$13 with $\mathfrak{P}$46) (see the critical apparatus of NA[26] and my 1990 book for discussions about these passages).

However, several significant Oxyrhynchian readings that have been rejected by NA[26] could very well reflect the original text. Some of the readings I have in mind are explained in chapter 10 (see Luke 22:43–44; John 1:34; 1 Cor. 7:40; 1 Thess. 5:9; Heb. 3:2; 12:3).

Chapter Six

Papyri Hidden in Jars: The Chester Beatty Papyri ($\mathfrak{P}$45, $\mathfrak{P}$46, $\mathfrak{P}$47) and The Coptos Papyri ($\mathfrak{P}$4, $\mathfrak{P}$64, $\mathfrak{P}$67)

On November 17, 1931, the *London Times* announced the discovery of twelve manuscripts said to have been found in a Coptic graveyard, stowed away in jars—eight manuscripts of the Old Testament, three of the New Testament, and one noncanonical text (Enoch). This was a sensational discovery—one just as monumental as the discovery of the Dead Sea Scrolls, which were found about twenty years later in jars in the Qumran caves. The eight manuscripts containing portions of the Greek Old Testament are as follows: two manuscripts of Genesis (one from the third century, another from the fourth), one of Numbers and Deuteronomy (second century), one of Ezekiel and Esther (third century), one of Isaiah (third century), one of Jeremiah (late second century), one of Daniel (third century), and one of Ecclesiasticus (fourth century). The three Greek New Testament manuscripts said to be found in the Coptic graveyard were the

71

earliest manuscripts to contain large portions of the New Testament text. The first manuscript, 𝔓45 (late second or early third century), is a codex of the four Gospels and Acts; the second, 𝔓46 (late first or early second century), is a codex of the Pauline Epistles; and the third, 𝔓47 (third century), is a codex of Revelation.

We know that both the Old Testament and New Testament manuscripts were produced by Christians because all are codexes (as opposed to rolls) and all display *nomina sacra*. This Christian library of Greek biblical texts was quite full: Genesis (two copies), Numbers, Deuteronomy, Isaiah, Jeremiah, Ezekiel, Daniel, Esther, Ecclesiasticus, the Gospels, Acts, the Pauline Epistles, and Revelation—plus Enoch, Melito, and apocryphal Ezekiel. Not one of the manuscripts was written in Coptic (although there are a few old Fayumic Coptic glosses written in the margin of the Isaiah manuscript).

Several scribes were responsible for producing the manuscripts; there is no paleographic indication that one particular scribe worked on more than one manuscript. Some of the manuscripts are the work of professional scribes—namely, the Numbers–Deuteronomy manuscript, 𝔓46 (the Pauline Epistles), the Isaiah manuscript, and the Jeremiah fragment. The Daniel manuscript and 𝔓45 (Gospels and Acts) may have also been done by professionals—at least, they display the reformed documentary hand. The smaller Genesis manuscript was also written in a documentary hand. The other manuscripts are not as well written, calligraphically speaking (Kenyon 1933–58: 1.13–14).

The manuscripts were purchased by Chester Beatty, an American living in Scotland, and by the University of Michigan from a Cairo dealer in different batches. Beatty purchased ten leaves of the Pauline Epistles and the University of Michigan purchased six leaves of the same manuscript (both in 1930–31). The University of Michigan acquired twenty-four more leaves in the winter of 1932–33. The ten leaves in the Beatty collection were first published in fascicle 3 of *The Chester Beatty Papyri* (1936) and the thirty leaves in the Michigan collection were published in 1935 by H. A. Sanders in *A Third-Century Papyrus Codex of the Epistles of Paul*. Soon after this publication, Beatty announced that he had obtained forty-six more leaves of the same manuscript. Through collaboration, the entire manuscript (eighty-six leaves) was published in 1936.

Henry A. Sanders elaborates (1935: 13) on the significance of the Coptic graveyard find:

> If, as is currently gossiped in Egypt, these papyri were found in a Coptic graveyard, we must think of them as belonging to a definite period, viz. that of the use of this graveyard as the place of burial of some Coptic monastery. Unfortunately, we do not know that all were found in one grave, though the presumption is in favor of that. Either fragmentary, and so worthless, manuscripts were buried with some dignitary of the monastery because he loved them, in which case there may have been several such burials in successive generations, or there was but one burial of all the remaining Greek books in the monastery upon the death of the last member of the group who used Greek. The life of a manuscript on papyrus was not long, when in use. Therefore, if all of the Greek manuscripts of the monastery were buried at one time, they should belong within a century, or approximately that, of each other.

Though it is possible that the manuscripts came from a Coptic graveyard, it is more likely that this designation was merely a fabrication created by the Egyptian diggers so as not to reveal the exact site of the discovery. Frederick Kenyon, the scholar who was responsible for publishing all the Chester Beatty manuscripts, writes (1937: 112):

> The circumstances of the find have never been fully revealed; indeed they are known only to the natives who made it, and their statements, for obvious reasons, are not very dependable. The first reports spoke of the district of the Fayum, to the west of the Nile; but information given to Dr. Carl Schmidt was to the effect that the actual site was on the opposite side of the river, near the remains of the ancient city Aphroditopolis.

Carl Schmidt was told (a few years after the discovery—in 1933) that the manuscripts were found in a pitcher in the ruins of a church or monastery near Aphroditopolis (modern Atfih). Furthermore, Schmidt's trusted Egyptian contact person indicated that these papyri could not have come from Upper Egypt, in view of the group of dealers from whom they came.[1]

---

1. See Schmidt 1931: 292–93; 1933: 225. Roberts (1979: 7) also records Schmidt's version of the finds: "Carl Schmidt was told in 1934 that the Chester Beatty papyri had been found in a pitcher . . . in the ruins of a church or monastery near Atfih (Aphroditopolis)."

Jews were known to put scrolls containing Scripture in pitchers or jars in order to preserve them. The Dead Sea Scrolls found in jars in the Qumran caves are a celebrated example of this. The Beatty papyri were very likely part of a Christian library, hidden in jars to be preserved from confiscation during the Diocletian persecution. Several years after the initial publication of these manuscripts, Kenyon wrote (1958: 116) that the find "presumably represents the library of some early Christian church."

Schofield suggests (1936: 7) that the manuscripts were found in a monastery that had been built by the monastics who followed Anthony, the founder of Egyptian monasticism. But this is unlikely because Anthony and his followers read the Scriptures in Coptic, not Greek (Metzger 1977: 104–5). What would they be doing with Greek manuscripts of the Old Testament and New Testament? (Of course, it is possible, as suggested by Sanders, that the Greek manuscripts were buried with the last member of the monastery to use Greek.) However, it seems more likely that the manuscripts came from a church and were hidden during the Diocletian persecution.

E. G. Kilpatrick believes that the Beatty manuscripts constituted a church library (somewhere in the Fayum) that survived the Diocletian persecution. This library of Greek biblical codexes "may be said to date before the persecution of Diocletian, when the Roman government required Christians to surrender their Scriptures. Somehow or other this Christian biblical library came through the storm intact or almost intact" (Kilpatrick 1963: 38).

The Christians never returned for these treasures, but we have them today. Need one point out how this scenario parallels that of the Dead Sea Scrolls? Prior to the discovery of the Dead Sea Scrolls, the discovery of the Beatty papyri was the greatest biblical find of the twentieth century.

E. G. Turner, followed by C. H. Roberts, at one time suggested that the Beatty manuscripts came from Panopolis, conjecturing therefore that both the Beatty and Bodmer papyri came from the same site. James M. Robinson has shown this theory to be in error.[2]

---

2. Although most scholars say the Beatty collection came from the Fayum, Turner (1968: 52–53; 1980: 201) suggested that both the Chester Beatty papyri and the Bodmer papyri came from an ancient church library in Panopolis.

𝔓45 (Chester Beatty Papyrus I), 150–200

According to Kenyon, the order of books in the original, intact papyrus codex of 𝔓45 was probably as follows: Matthew, John, Luke, Mark, Acts (the so-called Western order). Since the manuscripts came to London from Egypt in separate portions, this cannot be fully affirmed; however, since Mark and Acts arrived together, it is a fair assumption. The manuscript contains Matthew 20:24–32; 21:13–19; 25:41–26:39; Mark 4:36–9:31; 11:27–12:28; Luke 6:31–7:7; 9:26–14:33; John 10:7–25; 10:30–11:10, 18–36, 42–57; Acts 4:27–17:17 (with many lacunae).

The scribe of 𝔓45 did not copy his exemplar letter by letter (as in 𝔓75), syllable by syllable (as in 𝔓66), or even word by word; he copied phrase by phrase. Colwell says (1965: 381; repr. p. 117): "The scribe does not actually copy words. He sees through the language to its idea content, and copies that—often in words of his own choosing, or in words rearranged as to order." The scribe of 𝔓45 produced his manuscript without any intention of exactly copying his exemplar. He exercised great freedom in harmonizing, smoothing out the language, and using

---

Turner noticed that from 1930 to 1960 several intact or nearly intact papyrus books were acquired by collectors: Chester Beatty, Martin Bodmer, the University of Mississippi, and the papyrological institutes of Cologny and Barcelona. Turner said that it was "an economical hypothesis that all these papyri, whether works of Greek literature, documents, or Christian texts, are from one source and constitute a unitary find." Turner pointed to another connection between the Beatty and Bodmer papyri that links them both to Panopolis: Papyrus Bodmer I has the *Iliad* 5–6 written on the verso and a land register (written in A.D. 208/209) containing local names from the Panopolite nome written on the recto. Papyrus Beatty Panopolis contains the letter books of the strategus of Panopolis in A.D. 298 and 300; its unique construction is the same as that of four other papyri discovered in Panopolis in 1887. Publications from Geneva/Cologny include a register of property in Panopolis (published by V. Martin in *Recherches de Papyri* 2:37–73) and a petition (Papyrus Leitourgia 10) from the citizens of Panopolis to the senate of Panopolis. In his essay on books in the Greco-Roman world written for the *Cambridge History of the Bible* (1970: 56), Roberts seemed to confirm Turner's thesis: "It is possible, though not proven, that the Chester Beatty and Bodmer codices may have formed part of a single church library, accumulated over two centuries or more, and eventually deposited, in the Jewish fashion, in a Geniza." Turner's thesis was proven wrong by Robinson, who showed that the Bodmer biblical papyri came from Abu Mana (see Robinson 1986: 2–3 and chap. 7 for additional discussion).

surrogates. He is most notorious for his excisions. He omitted adverbs, adjectives, nouns, participles, and entire phrases and clauses. In short he favored brevity and conciseness. For example, instead of Jesus saying, "I am the resurrection and the life," 𝔓45 has Jesus say, "I am the resurrection" (John 11:25).

There is no evidence that 𝔓45 was corrected by the scribe himself or by a *diorthōtēs*. The scribe, a penman who made few careless errors, exercised total freedom in making many intentional changes. He was not under any obligation to transcribe the words of his exemplar faithfully. As a result, his text is a paraphrastic condensation of his exemplar. Thus, 𝔓45 is a paramount example of the "free" kind of text that existed in the second century. It, therefore, does not provide a good witness to the original text—especially in the Gospels. In the Book of Acts, however, the text is less free and more reliable.

Some later manuscripts show marked affinities with 𝔓45 in the Gospel of Mark. 𝔓45 and W have 67% agreement in the Gospel of Mark (Kenyon 1933–58: 2.xii); *f*1, 28, and Origen show general agreement with 𝔓45. Thus, it is safe to say that 𝔓45, *f*1, 28, W, and Origen form a textual group (Ayuso 1935). They provide an important witness to the early text when considered in conjunction with other witnesses. Their witness alone to a particular variant—unsupported by other early witnesses—is usually not very reliable.

As is explained in chapter 9, the testimony of 𝔓45 was far more often rejected than received in the formulation of NA²⁶. Nonetheless, there were a few instances in which the testimony of 𝔓45 was effective in making a change in the text. Some of the more noteworthy passages are as follows: Matthew 26:20; Mark 6:23; Luke 10:38, 42; John 10:16; 11:45 (see the critical apparatus of NA²⁶ and my 1990 book for discussions on these passages). But there are some readings supported by 𝔓45 that are worthy of inclusion in the text (for examples, see Luke 10:21 and 11:14 in chap. 10).

𝔓46 (Chester Beatty Papyrus II), ca. 85–150

Codex 𝔓46 contains most of Paul's epistles (excluding the pastorals), in this order: Romans (5:17–6:14; 8:15–15:9; 15:11–16:27), Hebrews, 1 Corinthians (minus 16:23–24), 2 Corinthians (minus 13:14), Ephesians, Galatians, Philippians,

Colossians, 1 Thessalonians (1:1; 1:9–2:3; 5:5–9, 23–28), with minor lacunae in each of the books.

The position of Hebrews immediately following Romans shows that Hebrews was considered a Pauline epistle. It also shows that 𝔓46 was not indigenous to Rome (where Hebrews was not accepted as Pauline until the fourth century), but to Alexandria (where Hebrews was accepted as Pauline from a very early date). 𝔓46 is also the only manuscript to have the doxology (usually appearing in Rom. 16:25–27) at the end of chapter 15—thereby giving "witness to a text of the letter which lacked chapter 16" (Bruce 1988: 140 n. 18). 𝔓46 was indeed a very early copy of the Pauline corpus because its exemplar would have had Romans 16 as an appended chapter; as mentioned previously, it is likely that the original compiler of the Pauline corpus was the first one to append Romans 16 to the rest of the epistle.

Zuntz (1953: 11) dates 𝔓46 at 200, but mentions that Ulrich Wilcken, director of the Vienna library and founder of *Archiv für Papyrusforschung,* dated the work earlier in the second century. Kim (1988) dates it 85–90 (see pp. 30–31). Thus, it is safe to date the codex somewhere between 85 and 150.

The close relationship between 𝔓46 and 𝔓13 is noteworthy. Out of 86 variant readings, there are 71 agreements, with only 17 disagreements—an 82% rate of agreement (Kenyon 1933–58: 3/sup. xv). And the amount of agreement is higher when one considers that 𝔓13 has 5 single readings and 𝔓46 has 6 single readings (Sanders 1935: 18, 34). There are other noteworthy similarities between 𝔓13 and 𝔓46: (1) The two manuscripts have similar stichometry. (2) The copyists of both manuscripts made similar use of double points for punctuation. They agree in the placement of punctuation 34 times and disagree only 20 times. (3) The pagination of both documents is strikingly similar. The page numbers of 𝔓46 show correspondence with the column numbers of 𝔓13. For example, 𝔓13 begins column 47 with Hebrews 2:14; 𝔓46 has Hebrews 2:14 on page 44. 𝔓13 begins column 62 with Hebrews 10:8; 𝔓46 must have begun Hebrews 10:6 on page 61. (4) The pagination of both manuscripts indicates that Romans immediately preceded Hebrews (Sanders 1935: 18, 34).[3] No other extant manuscripts of the Pauline Epistles have this order.

3. In 𝔓13, the following columns are marked: 47–50, 63–65, 67–69.

The scribe of 𝔓46 was a professional scribe who worked in a scriptorium. We know this because several of the books are marked with stichometric notations (1,000 stichoi for Romans, 700 for Hebrews, 316 for Ephesians, 375 for Galatians, 225 for Philippians)—a practice employed only by professional scribes who earned their wage per stichos. We also know that 𝔓46 was done in a scriptorium because several correctors worked on this manuscript. Unfortunately, the original scribe performed his task too hastily and thereby created a number of scribal blunders. He himself made some corrections, but not throughout the entire manuscript. In defense of the original scribe, it should be said that it was not unusual for a scribe to not correct a manuscript—knowing that was the task of the *diorthōtēs* or even the purchaser. Often, the *diorthōtēs* would correct the copy against another exemplar to ensure accuracy. The scribe who made his own manuscript and then corrected it himself would not do as good a job as another person. (The same principle is operative in modern publishing houses—in which proofreaders and backreaders are employed to check over the work of an editor or an author.)

Besides the original scribe who made some minor corrections, there was another corrector, who may have also added the stichometric notes and pagination. According to Zuntz (1953: 252–54), this is the hand of the *ex officio* corrector who, still in the scriptorium, applied the finishing touches to the work of the scribe. According to C. H. Roberts (cited in Zuntz 1953: 253–54), the third corrector—a scribe in the late third century—corrected a few places whose wording struck him as incorrect. Either he or another scribe inserted reading marks, in Romans and Hebrews only, to aid the reading of the text in church meetings (Sanders 1935: 17). This scribe, very likely a lector, was the last scribe to touch the manuscript before it was hidden away in a jar.

The three most comprehensive and significant studies of the textual character of 𝔓46 were done by Kenyon (1933–58, vol. 3/sup.), Sanders (1935), and Zuntz (1953). Both Kenyon and Sanders affirm the Alexandrian textual character of 𝔓46, noting especially its affinities with B. According to Kenyon's tabulation (1933–58: 3/sup. xv–xvi), 𝔓46 and B have the following percentages of agreement: Romans (66%), 1 Corinthians (75%), 2 Corinthians (78%), Galatians (74%), Ephesians (84%), Philip-

pians (73%), Colossians (78%), and Hebrews (79%). 𝔓46 also
has an affinity with ℵ (but the percentages of agreement are
about 5% lower for each book). Note the extremely high agreement in Ephesians and Hebrews; the lower agreement in
Romans is because B is noted for its Western tendencies in
Romans. 𝔓46 also shows great affinity with other witnesses.
Zuntz affirms (1953: 265) an early eastern group of manuscripts—𝔓46, B, 1739, Coptic Sahidic, Coptic Boharic, Clement,
and Origen—for the Pauline corpus. The relationship between
𝔓46 and 1739 is noteworthy because 1739 is a tenth-century
manuscript that was copied from a fourth-century manuscript
of excellent quality. According to its colophon, the scribe of
1739 for the Pauline Epistles followed a manuscript from Caesarea in the library of Pamphilus, which contained an Origenian
text (Zuntz 1953: 71–78; Metzger 1968: 65). The three manuscripts form a clear textual line: from 𝔓46 (early second century) to B (early fourth century) to 1739 (tenth century). Zuntz
says (1953: 83):

> Within the wider affinities of the "Alexandrian" tradition, the
> Vaticanus is now seen to stand out as a member of a group with
> 𝔓46 and the pre-ancestor of 1739. The early date of the text-form
> which this group preserves is fixed by its oldest member and its
> high quality is borne out by many striking instances. B is in fact
> a witness for a text, not of c. A.D. 360, but of c. A.D. 200.[4]

The most thorough study on the text of 𝔓46 was done by
Zuntz. Quick to point out the many scribal blunders found in
𝔓46, Zuntz was just as eager to demonstrate (1953: 247, 212–13)
that 𝔓46 is a representative of a text of the superior, early-
Alexandrian type:

> The excellent quality of the text represented by our oldest manu-
> script, 𝔓46, stands out again. As so often before, we must here be
> careful to distinguish between the very poor work of the scribe
> who penned it and the basic text which he so poorly rendered.
> 𝔓46 abounds with scribal blunders, omissions, and also addi-
> tions. In some of them the scribe anticipated the errors of later
> copyists; in some other instances he shares an older error; but

---

4. In light of Kim's 1988 dating of 𝔓46, Zuntz's final sentence would now
have to be amended: "B is in fact a witness for a text of the late first century or
early second century."

the vast majority are his own uncontested property. Once they have been discarded, there remains a text of outstanding (though not absolute) purity.

His impressions of 𝔓46 led Zuntz to generalize (1953: 262) about the philological acumen of Alexandrian scribes in the second and third centuries:

> The consistent effort to eliminate [i.e., Western errors] is evidence of the existence and the effects of a Christian critical philology as early as c. A.D. 200; a philology conscious of its aims and sure of its methods. Those early critics committed errors; they sometimes admitted spurious readings. Some of these errors . . . were corrected as the critical work proceeded; others were carried on; still others were added in the course of this very tradition. Hence the modern critic must always be prepared to trace an original reading in that tradition which the "Alexandrian" critics combated. But he owes it to these early colleagues that he can do his work at all and that, in spite of a widespread tendency towards looseness and corruption, the original text has, to a large extent, survived.

𝔓46 is a prime example of the kind of early Alexandrian text that—discounting scribal blunders—preserves nearly all the original wording of Paul's inspired writings. Birdsall affirms this when he says (1970: 350) that 𝔓46, B, and 1739 "often attest a text acceptable upon the principles of rational criticism as original."

Where there was textual variation, the testimony of 𝔓46 was accepted into NA²⁶ in only 68% of the occurrences. In about 35 instances, 𝔓46 was instrumental in creating a change from N²⁵ to NA²⁶. Some of the more noteworthy passages are as follows: Romans 8:21; 1 Corinthians 10:9; 13:3; 2 Corinthians 2:1; 3:9; Ephesians 1:14; 3:9; Philippians 1:14; 3:13; Colossians 3:4; Hebrews 3:6; 4:2; 11:11 (see the critical apparatus of NA²⁶ and my 1990 book for discussions on these passages). The testimony of 𝔓46 was rejected 32% of the time by NA²⁶. Often, 𝔓46 and B were rejected together, when it is very likely that they witness to the original wording. Some of the more noteworthy rejections—which I believe belong in the text—are commented on in chapter 10 (see discussions on Rom. 8:28; 1 Cor. 10:2; 2 Cor. 1:10, 12; Eph. 1:1; 4:28; Col. 3:6; Heb. 12:3).

℘47 (Chester Beatty Papyrus III), Third Century

℘47 contains Revelation 9:10–17:2. According to Kenyon (1933–58: 3.xii), the writing of ℘47 is "rather rough in character, thick in formation, and with no pretensions to calligraphy. . . . [Nonetheless], the writing is generally correct." ℘47 agrees with א, a group that is second in textual fidelity to the A–C group. This has been affirmed by the extensive studies of Josef Schmid (1955–56) in the text of the Book of Revelation. According to Schmid, there are four groups of manuscripts for the Book of Revelation (listed here in descending order of fidelity):

Best text: A, C, 2344, Oecumenis's commentary
2d: ℘47, א, Origen
3d: Koine Majority/K^m
4th: Andreas's commentary

Of ℘47 and א Birdsall says (1970: 352), "While often sharing good ancient readings with other witnesses such as A, [℘47 and א show by themselves] few acceptable ones, and many signs of ancient corruption, frequently in attempts to simplify by abbreviation." The testimony of ℘47 has made little impact on NA[26], being rejected 85% of the time. However, there are a few instances in which ℘47 (with other manuscripts) might very likely preserve the original wording and should be reflected in NA[26] (see comments on Rev. 14:3 and 15:3 in chap. 10).

The Coptos Papyri (℘4, ℘64, ℘67), ca. 200

A manuscript containing two treatises by Philo and portions of Matthew and Luke was discovered in Coptos (modern Qift), Egypt, on the east bank of the Nile, by Vincent Scheil during his expedition to Upper Egypt in 1880. Jean Merell describes the history of this manuscript (Merell 1938: 5–7; translation provided by Richard Comfort; see also Scheil 1892: 113–15):

> Scheil told me last June that, in 1891, having purchased in Luxor a codex including two treatises of Philo of Alexandria, he was fortunate to find the fragments of our biblical papyrus.
> The papyrus was found at Coptos (Upper Egypt) in 1880. Since it was obviously considered at the time to be something very

valuable, it was enclosed and concealed in a niche. (The hollow sound of the thick, high wall at this point was noteworthy.) In opening the area, one found in this secret place the two treatises of Philo of Alexandria. The entire document, in a well-known format, almost square, in 8″ Arabic books, was bound together in a leather cover, with a small tongue and cord (also in leather) wrapped around the cover. In the hiding place, the book must have been compressed in the space, the mortar was encrusted on the outside; the pages were tightly pressed together in a mass and, in addition, they were also fastened to each other by a quantity of small grains of sand, produced by an ancient condensation occurring in the vegetal tissue.

After the forty-fourth sheet, in the form of a wad, I believe, and in order to fill the space provided by the cover, there were several fragments of sheets stuck together, one of them containing the Κατὰ Μαθθαῖον and the others having the fragments of St. Luke.

According to Roberts (1979: 8), 𝔓4 was used as stuffing for the leather binding of the Philo codex. Roberts also adds the extra detail that the manuscript had been in a jar.

No portion of Matthew, besides the title Κατὰ Μαθθαῖον ([The Gospel] according to Matthew), was discovered with the portions of Luke. However in later years, two separate portions of Matthew were published by independent sources. 𝔓64 was published by Colin Roberts in 1953 and 𝔓67 was published by P. Roca-Puig in 1957.[5] Roberts later realized that 𝔓64 and 𝔓67 were two parts of the same manuscript and then confirmed this with Roca-Puig. The two scholars then published an article in 1961 in which Roca-Puig gave a full presentation of the entire manuscript and Roberts explained how he had discovered that 𝔓64 and 𝔓67 were part of the same manuscript. Still later, Roberts came to the conclusion that 𝔓4 belonged to the same manuscript as 𝔓64/67 (see Roberts 1979: 13). Thus, 𝔓64 and 𝔓67 constitute parts of 𝔓4, the Κατὰ Μαθθαῖον manuscript.

The editor of the Philo treatises demonstrated that the text derived from an archetype once in the library of Caesarea in Palestine (cited in Roberts 1979: 8). This library, begun by Pamphilus (who was martyred in the Diocletian persecution of 307)

---

5. 𝔓64 was purchased in 1901 in Luxor, Egypt, just south of Coptos. Roberts indicated that the Magdalen library purchased more portions of the same manuscript in successive years but that none of the portions are now extant.

and then given to the church in Caesarea, included several books that had belonged to Origen, who had come to Caesarea in 231 and instituted a center of Christian scholarship (including a scriptorium). Two of the priceless treasures in Pamphilus's library were the original copies of Origen's Hexapla and Tetrapla. Eusebius took care of Pamphilus's library after it was given to the church in Caesarea and he used these resources to compose his *Ecclesiastical History*. The Philo treatises could have been written in Caesarea or copied from an exemplar that came from Caesarea. So also, the New Testament fragments (Roberts 1963: 12–15). If so, the New Testament fragments came from an early Caesarean archetype. But it is also possible that the New Testament portions came from an Egyptian archetype and were subsequently used as padding by an inhabitant of Coptos for the Philo codex. Because of the title Κατὰ Μαθθαῖον, it is probable that the codex that originally contained 𝔓64/67 and 𝔓4 very likely had all four Gospels—with the titles Κατὰ Μαθθαῖον, Κατὰ Μᾶρκον, Κατὰ Λουκᾶν, Κατὰ Ἰωάννην—which would make it the first known codex to have this format.

The manuscript 𝔓4/64/67 is a thoroughgoing literary production penned by a trained scribe. The text is divided into sections according to a system found in 𝔓75 and also in some great fourth-century manuscripts (i.e., ℵ and B). Furthermore, this manuscript exhibits three different positions for punctuation, as well as omission and quotation signs (in a system similar to that found in 𝔓66). The textual fidelity of this manuscript is very sound; quite specifically, 𝔓4 antedates B (in Luke) and 𝔓64/67 antedates ℵ (in Matthew), yet is purer and closer to the original.

Where there are significant variant readings, 𝔓4/64/67 usually affirms the text of NA[26] and UBS[3] (e.g., Matt. 5:22, 25; Luke 1:78; 3:22; 6:1; see the discussion concerning these verses in my 1990 book).

Chapter Seven

Papyri from a Monastery Library: The Bodmer Biblical Papyri (𝔓66, 𝔓72, 𝔓75)

The most exciting and significant discovery of biblical manuscripts since the Dead Sea Scrolls is that of the Dishna Papers, several of which are known as the Bodmer biblical papyri and a few of which are also in the Chester Beatty collection. The early New Testament manuscripts known as the Bodmer papyri were purchased by Martin Bodmer (founder of the Bodmer Library of World Literature in Cologny, a suburb of Geneva) from a dealer in Cairo, Egypt, in the 1950s and 1960s.

The place of discovery in Egypt was not revealed for over twenty years. Scholars were guessing that the discovery of the ancient manuscripts was in the area between Panopolis (modern Akmim) and Thebes because (1) Papyrus Bodmer I, a land register (written A.D. 208/209), contained local names from the Panopolite nome written on the recto of an *Iliad* manuscript; (2) several of the manuscripts in the Bodmer collection are written in Coptic Sahidic, an Egyptian dialect used in southern

85

Egypt (especially in the area between Panopolis and Thebes); and (3) Papyrus Bodmer VII–VIII ($\mathfrak{P}$72) evidences the work of Coptic scribes in the vicinity of Thebes (see comments below under $\mathfrak{P}$72). Kilpatrick, writing in 1963 (34), said that these factors "point to the southern half of Egypt and within this area to a locality between Panopolis and Thebes."

In recent years James Robinson, an expert in the Nag Hammadi manuscripts, was able to pinpoint the place of discovery while attempting to find out where the Nag Hammadi manuscripts came from. The Bodmer biblical papyri were discovered seven years after the Nag Hammadi codexes and in close proximity—in the Dishna Plain, east of the Nile River (Dishna is midway between Panopolis and Thebes). In 1945 the Nag Hammadi manuscripts were found in Jabal al-Ṭārif, just north of Chenoboskia, which was near Nag Hammadi, the city where the discovery was first reported. In 1952 the Bodmer papyri were found in Jabal Abu Mana, which is also located just north of the Dishna Plain, twelve kilometers east of Jabal al-Ṭārif (see Robinson 1986: 4–5; Robinson 1979; Van Elderen 1979).

The following description of the Bodmer discovery is adapted from the story told by James Robinson, who did an extensive, firsthand investigation of both the Nag Hammadi and Dishna discoveries (see Robinson 1986: 11–25).

In broad daylight a Muslim peasant named Ḥasan (presumably from Abu Mana Bahari) went out near the cliffs beyond the limits of arable land looking for *sabakh* (fertilizer), but this may have been an excuse for seeking treasure. While digging with a mattock, Ḥasan found some ancient books, but he was not particularly impressed with his find. He gave some of the books away to bystanders and took the rest home (presumably in a jar). The villagers knew of the discovery, which occurred around the time of the fall of King Farouk (July 23, 1952). Not knowing the value of these ancient Greek and Coptic manuscripts, Ḥasan burned some of the leaves—to light a water pipe or just to smell the fragrance of burning papyrus. Ḥasan attempted to barter the papyri codexes for cigarettes or oranges, but the villagers were not interested—deeming the books worthless.

Word of the discovery soon reached communication and trade centers outside of the village. Middlemen emerged who wanted to sell the papyri to antiquity dealers in Alexandria or

Cairo. The first purchaser of the Bodmer papyri was a goldsmith from Dishna. The goldsmith's son was a teacher at the same parochial school as the former owner of Codex III in the Nag Hammadi manuscripts, which had been sold to the Coptic Museum. When the goldsmith's son showed the papyrus to the Coptic Museum, it was nearly confiscated. From then on, the goldsmith was virtually under house arrest. But the papyri were safe from police search because they had been put in the house of a Coptic priest, who then became a coconspirator in the clandestine operation to traffic the manuscripts to Cairo. It took the goldsmith three years to sell off the papyri—at a very good price (due to the good market of the Nag Hammadi manuscripts). A Cairo dealer, Phocion Tano, bought and sold both Nag Hammadi manuscripts and Dishna manuscripts—many to Martin Bodmer of Geneva, Switzerland, some to Chester Beatty of Dublin, Ireland, and a few to other buyers.

The collection is as follows (adapted from Robinson 1990):

I. Bodmer Manuscripts
  A. Greek Biblical Writings
    1. II: Gospel of John ($\mathfrak{P}$66)
    2. VII–IX: 1–2 Peter, Jude ($\mathfrak{P}$72), and Psalms 33–34
    3. XIV–XV: Luke and John ($\mathfrak{P}$75)
    4. XVII: Acts, James, 1–2 Peter, Jude ($\mathfrak{P}$74; seventh century—this manuscript did not come from the same find as the rest of the manuscripts)
    5. XXIV: Psalms 17–118
    6. XLVI: Daniel
  B. Greek Christian Writings
    1. V: the Nativity of Mary
    2. X–XII: the apocryphal correspondence of Paul to the Corinthians, Odes of Solomon, liturgical hymn, Apology of Phileas
    3. XIII: homily of Melitus
    4. XLV–XLVI: Suzanna, Moral Exhortations
    5. XXIX–XXXVIII: Codex Visionum
  C. Coptic Biblical and Christian Writings
    1. III: John, Genesis
    2. VI: Proverbs

      3. XVI: Exodus

      4. XVIII: Deuteronomy

      5. XIX: Matthew, Romans

      6. XXI: Joshua (divided with the Beatty collection)

      7. XXII: Jeremiah 40–52, Lamentations, Epistle of Jeremy, Baruch (divided with the University of Mississippi)

      8. XXIII: Isaiah 47–66

      9. XL: Song of Songs

     10. XLI: Acts of Paul

     11. XLII: 2 Corinthians

     12. XLIII: Apocryphon

     13. XLIV: Daniel

  D. Literary Writings

      1. I: Homer's *Iliad*, Books 5–6

      2. IV: Menander's *Le Dyscolos*

      3. XX: *Martyrium*

      4. XXVII: Thucydides

      5. XXVIII: Satyr play

      6. XLVIII: fragments of Homer's *Iliad*

      7. XLIX: Homer's *Odyssey*

II. Beatty Manuscripts

  A. Greek

      1. Greek Grammar, Greco-Latin Lexicon of Romans, 2 Corinthians, Galatians, Ephesians (Beatty 1499)

      2. Psalms 72–88 (Papyrus Beatty XIII)

      3. Psalms 2, 26, 31 (Papyrus Beatty XIV)

      4. Legal documents from Panopolis (Beatty 2554)

  B. Coptic

      1. Apocalypse of Elijah (Beatty 2018)

III. Manuscripts in Other Collections

  A. Melito of Sardis's *On the Passover*, 2 Maccabees 5:27–7:41, 1 Peter, Jonah, homily or hymn (Crosby-Schoyen Codex) [Greek or Coptic?]

  B. Scholia to the *Odyssey* I (Papyrus Colon 906)

  C. Achilleus Tatios (Papyrus Colon 901)

  D. A philosophical treatise (Papyrus Colon 903)

E. Cicero's *In Catilinam*, Psalmus Responsorius, Greek liturgical text, *Alcestis*—all in Latin except Greek liturgical text (Papyrus Barcinonenses 149–161 and Papyrus Duke L)

F. Luke, John, Mark in Coptic Sahidic (Papyrus Palau Ribes 181–183)

IV. Copies of Letters from Pachomian Abbots
   A. Pachomius
      1. Letter 11b in Coptic Sahidic (Papyrus Bodmer XXXIX)
      2. Letters 9a, 9b, 10, 11b in Coptic Sahidic (Beatty 2556)
      3. Letters 1–3, 7, 10, 11a in Greek (Beatty MS W.145 and Papyrus Köln 174)
      4. Letter 8 in Coptic Sahidic (Papyrus Köln agypt 8)
      5. Letter 9 in Coptic Sahidic (Papyrus Köln agypt 9)
   B. Theodore
      1. Letter 2 in Coptic Sahidic (Beatty 1486)
      2. Second copy of Letter 2 in Coptic Sahidic (private collection)
   C. Horiesios
      1. Letter 3 in Coptic Sahidic (Beatty 1494)
      2. Letter 4 in Coptic Sahidic (Beatty 1495)

Some of the Greek manuscripts listed above are dated in the second century (𝔓66, 𝔓75, Bodmer papyri X–XII), but most of them are third or fourth century. The Coptic manuscripts date from the fourth century to the seventh century. The complete collection shows that the monks used Greek biblical texts and other Christian writings (dated from the second to fourth centuries), Coptic biblical texts (dated from the fourth and fifth centuries), and Coptic Christian writings (dated from the fourth to seventh centuries)—especially the letters of their founding abbots Pachomius and Theodore. These manuscripts were buried probably in the seventh century near the cliffs of Jabal Abu Mana, a place used by the monks for the burial of their dead (Robinson 1990: 2–6, 19–21).

It is quite likely that all these manuscripts were part of a library of a Pachomian monastery. Within a few kilometers of Jabal Abu Mana lies the ruins of the ancient basilica of

Pachomius (in Fāw Qiblī). Pachomius (287–346) brought monasticism to this area around A.D. 320. By the time of his death, there were thousands of monks in eleven monasteries in a radius of sixty miles along the Nile River. A century later there were nearly fifty thousand monks in the area. As part of their daily regimen, these monks read and memorized the Scriptures—especially the New Testament and Psalms. Pachomius himself took an active role in this practice in that he read the Scriptures aloud to his first congregation (i.e., he was the lector). As Pachomius knew both Coptic and Greek (as did other monks in his monasteries), some of the monks must have read the Scriptures in both languages. Of course, more monks read Coptic than Greek, and with the passing of time (beginning in the fifth century) almost all read only Coptic.

Because the library in the Pachomian monastery could not have started until after 320, all earlier manuscripts—especially the New Testament papyri—must have been produced in other scriptoria and given to the library. The manuscripts dated in the fourth and fifth centuries are of two types: those that were the result of poor craftsmanship and those that appear to have been done professionally. It is therefore quite likely that the monks produced some of their own poorly made books and that they were given professionally made manuscripts from an outside scriptorium—very likely from Alexandria.

It appears that the early biblical manuscripts (as well as the later ones that show the work of professionalism) came from Alexandria. These manuscripts were probably given to the monastery by Athanasius or Theodore. Pachomius greatly respected Bishop Athanasius of Alexandria and maintained a good relationship with him. During his third exile (356–361), Athanasius hid in Thebaid caves and monasteries and was very likely supported and supplied by Pachomius's followers.

Athanasius had ordained Pachomius to the presbyterate (in 329) and continually given his blessings to his community; the Pachomian community, in return, revered Athanasius, the champion of orthodoxy. It would have been natural for this community to use the type of New Testament text produced in Alexandria and authorized by Athanasius, who was the first Egyptian bishop to exercise his authority over all the Egyptian churches. In this regard Aland and Aland (1987: 65) write:

Athanasius, the powerful bishop of Alexandria, whose authority was felt far beyond the borders of Egypt as early as 328, governed his church with a tightly centralized administrative structure. We do not know precisely what manuscript he designated for use as a model, but it must have been of the type represented by Codex Vaticanus or 𝔓75.

𝔓75, part of the Pachomian collection (I.A.3 in the outline above) and the precursor to Codex Vaticanus, was found in Abu Mana, most likely brought there from Alexandria. Other manuscripts, much like 𝔓75, remaining in Alexandria would have served as exemplars for Vaticanus (a production of the Alexandrian scriptorium)—unless, of course, all the New Testament manuscripts had been obliterated in Alexandria during the Diocletian persecution, in which case the post-Diocletian Alexandrian church made use of manuscripts from other cities— manuscripts like 𝔓13 from Oxyrhynchus, 𝔓46 from the Fayum, and 𝔓75 from Abu Mana. Either way, the text type originated from Alexandria.

If it was not Athanasius who donated 𝔓75 to the Pachomius library, it could have been Theodore, a lector who had come to Pachomius from the church in Alexandria. Theodore was well received by Pachomius (even inspiring Pachomius to learn Greek) and made steward of all those who came to the monastery from Alexandria and other Greek-speaking regions (*Life of Pachomias* 94–95). Quite interestingly, one of the fourth-century manuscripts found in the Dishna Papers has a Greek verb conjugation chart and grammatical aids for reading Paul's epistles in Greek. This may have been the actual work of Theodore who provided this help for those learning Greek— including Pachomius. The fourth-century copies of Homer's *Iliad* and Menander may have also belonged to Theodore.

As lector in the church of Alexandria, it was Theodore's task to keep copies of the biblical texts. He may have brought these copies with him or made arrangements for other copies to be sent from Alexandria so that his fellow Greek-speaking ascetics would have copies of the Scripture to read and memorize. If the monastery had a scriptorium, which seems doubtful, Theodore would have been the one to oversee the production of books. In this position, he could have exerted the influences of Alexandrian scriptoral practices.

𝔓66 (Bodmer Papyrus II), 150–175

𝔓66 preserves most of the Gospel of John (1:1–6:11; 6:35–14:26; 14:29–30; 15:2–26; 16:2–4, 6–7; 16:10–20:20; 20:22–23; 20:25–21:9). Because of its construction, we are certain that the manuscript originally contained only the Gospel of John. 𝔓66 is usually dated approximately 200, but Herbert Hunger, director of papyrological collections in the National Library at Vienna, dated it around 125–150 (see Hunger 1960).

The scribe of 𝔓66 wrote in increasingly larger print as he progressed through the book, in order to fill out the codex. The large print throughout indicates that it was written to be read aloud to a Christian congregation (Turner 1977: 84–86).

Various scholars who have studied the manuscript have indicated that 𝔓66 most likely was the product of a scriptorium. In particular, there are two features that point to this conclusion: the scribe's excellent calligraphy and the changes to the text made against a second *Vorlage* (exemplar). Colwell (1965: 382; repr. p. 118) says:

> 𝔓66 seems to reflect a scribe working with the intention of making a good copy, falling into careless errors, particularly the error of dropping a letter, syllable, a word, or even a phrase where it is doubled, but also under the control of some other person, or a second standard, so that the corrections which are made are usually corrections to a reading read by a number of other witnesses. Nine out of ten of the nonsense readings are corrected, and two out of three of all his singular readings. In short, 𝔓66 gives the impression of being the product of a scriptorium, i.e., a publishing house. It shows the supervision of a foreman, or of a scribe turned proofreader.

The copyist of 𝔓66 copied his exemplar syllable by syllable and in the process made many mistakes—nearly 450! But the manuscript was not left uncorrected. Scholars recognize that 𝔓66 was emended in three stages:

1. The scribe of 𝔓66 made some immediate corrections as he was producing his copy.
2. After the transcription of 𝔓66 was completed, a preliminary check of the manuscript was made (either by the scribe himself or by a more experienced colleague). This corrector was concerned with orthography, but

also had an interest in seeing that the sentences should read sensibly. (This is like proofreading a printed text before it goes to press.)

3. A second review of the manuscript was made with a greater concern for transcriptional accuracy. An exemplar (different from the first exemplar) was employed at this stage. Corrections were made in the direction of producing a text that is quite similar to N[25] (see Rhodes 1968).

Gordon Fee makes some further observations about the corrections that appear in 𝔓66. Fee believes that two exemplars were used in the making of 𝔓66—the second exemplar was not used for the original preparation of the manuscript, but for corrections only. In most instances, the scribe himself functioned as the corrector, making corrections in smaller print and with haste. Fee (1965: 253–54) writes:

> The scribe had recourse to another MS (or MSS) with which he compared his own completed MS and made some changes accordingly. . . . The scribe of 𝔓66, after copying from one MS, had opportunity at a later time to check his copy against another MS, with the result that in a number of instances he *chose* one reading over another and changed his MS.

For example, the original hand of 𝔓66 in John 11:33 reads, "He was agitated in [his] spirit and troubled in himself." This was corrected to read, "He was troubled in [his] spirit as [if] agitated"—which is also the reading in 𝔓45[vid], D, and some other witnesses. The correction undoubtedly presents an attempt to soften the statement about Jesus' agitation and anger.

Fee notes other instances in which it appears that a second hand may have been at work in correcting 𝔓66—through addition (e.g., John 13:19: ἀπ' ἄρτι λέγω ὑμῖν πρὸ) or deletion (marked by superior dots—as opposed to scraping out or crossing out, both of which were used by the original scribe). In many cases this corrector's deletions made the text more accurate: 7:39 (omit ἅγιον), 7:40 (omit πολλοὶ), 7:46 (omit ὡς οὗτος λαλεῖ ὁ ἄνθρωπος), 10:26 (omit καθὼς εἶπον ὑμῖν), and 14:4 (omit καὶ . . . οἴδατε). But the corrections are not thoroughgoing and therefore do not reflect any kind of scholarly recension. However, the corrected text is more akin to the Alexandrian tradition (Fee 1968: 57–75).

The textual relationships of 𝔓66 with other early manuscripts have been delineated by Fee (1968: 9–35) as follows:

1. In John 1–5, 𝔓66 has a close relationship with 𝔓75, B,
    and C. The highest agreement is with 𝔓75 (65.2%), and
    the agreement is even higher between 𝔓66ᶜ and 𝔓75
    (68.7%). Thus, in John 1–5, 𝔓66ᶜ and 𝔓75 are of the
    same textual family.
2. In John 6–7, 𝔓66 has a notable relationship with ℵ,
    which is Western in this portion. 𝔓66* agrees with ℵ*
    56.9%, and 𝔓66ᶜ agrees with ℵᶜ 63.4%.
3. In John 8–14, 𝔓66 has no distinguishable affinities but
    is clearly marked with a number of Byzantine-type
    readings.
4. In John 15–21, it is difficult to establish manuscript
    relationships because 𝔓75 does not contain this portion
    and because 𝔓66 has a great many gaps in this section.
    Nonetheless, it can be said that in John 19 𝔓66 is closer
    to B than to ℵ.

Overall, it can be said that 𝔓66 has the closest relationship to
𝔓75 and B (as well as C), but they are not in the same family
because 𝔓66 often fails to follow 𝔓75 and B where the two
show very clear textual relatedness. When 𝔓66 varies from the
Alexandrian tradition, it is in the direction of the Western text
(in John 6–7) or in the direction of Byzantine-type readings (in
John 14–18, 20–21). However, from John 8:39 to the end, 𝔓66
remains more closely related to 𝔓75 and B than to ℵ. Thus, one
could say that 𝔓66 is basically an Alexandrian text with Western and Byzantine-type infusions.

One can conclude that the scribe of 𝔓66 was not bent on preserving the best text in the sense of what John actually wrote,
but the best text in the sense of what reading made the most
sense or was the easiest—which was typical of the kind of
emendations that went into making the Byzantine text.
Furthermore, the scribe of 𝔓66 appears to have been new on
the job. He was an excellent calligrapher but in need of correction. He himself made many corrections, as did another corrector. These corrections, on the whole, made the text more

accurate and more akin to manuscripts like 𝔓75 and B. But the correcting process was not thorough—a phenomenon also observable in 𝔓46.

Given the shortcomings of 𝔓66, it still presents a reliable witness to many of the significant variant readings in the Gospel of John. Where there was textual variation among the manuscripts, the testimony of 𝔓66 (and/or 𝔓66ᶜ) was accepted about 75% of the time in NA²⁶. This is a high percentage. Nonetheless, the editors of NA²⁶ would have done better to accept some other significant readings supported by 𝔓66 (see John 4:1; 5:44; 7:53–8:11; 10:29; 13:2; 19:35; 20:31 in chap. 10).

𝔓72 (Papyrus Bodmer VII–VIII), Third Century

According to Michel Testuz (1959: 9), the editor of 𝔓72, this manuscript was very likely written for a rich member of the Christian community in Egypt for his own private library. The small size of the codex (15.5 cm × 14.2 cm) indicates that it was not produced for liturgical purposes. This codex contains all of 1 Peter, 2 Peter, and Jude; the same document contains the Nativity of Mary, the apocryphal correspondence of Paul to the Corinthians, the eleventh ode of Solomon, Melito's Homily on the Passover, a fragment of a hymn, the Apology of Phileas, and Psalms 33 and 34.

𝔓72 was probably not a product of the church's scriptorium since it is clearly produced for an individual. Because of a marginal note (on 2 Pet. 2:22) written in Coptic and the frequent confusion between gamma (γ) and kappa (κ), which is particularly localized at Thebes, Testuz (1959: 9) concludes that this was the place of writing. However, Kilpatrick (1963: 34) thinks the evidence points more precisely to a location between Panopolis and Thebes (i.e., Abu Mana).

Although four different scribes took part in making the codex, the same scribe produced the New Testament books, as is evidenced by the handwriting. Not the best of scribes, he committed many scribal blunders due to carelessness. However, if the scribal errors and singular readings due to carelessness are removed, the text appears to be of good quality (Kubo 1965: 17). According to Kubo's thorough study of 𝔓72 (which followed the methodology implemented by Zuntz for 𝔓46), 𝔓72 has the greatest affinity with B (73% agreement), followed by

1739 (62%), C (59%), 33 (58%), and A (57%). With these fig-
ures, $\mathfrak{P}$72 and B can be classified as having definite textual affinity (with over 70% agreement—a 10% margin over any other
manuscript). Kubo (1965: 154) states: "Where $\mathfrak{P}$72 and B agree
in their basic text, their common text is almost always superior to any other opposing combinations." And where $\mathfrak{P}$72 and
B differ, "$\mathfrak{P}$72 was seen to preserve more genuine readings than
B." Thus, $\mathfrak{P}$72 has a better text than B overall. This is especially
true in 1–2 Peter. In Jude, however, $\mathfrak{P}$72 is more idiosyncratic
and wild.[1]

Despite the excellent testimony of $\mathfrak{P}$72 in 1 Peter, where
there was textual variation, the editors of NA[26] adopted the
readings of $\mathfrak{P}$72 only 66% of the time. The testimony of $\mathfrak{P}$72
in 2 Peter was accepted 80% of the time. In Jude, however, $\mathfrak{P}$72
was followed only 38% of the time.

$\mathfrak{P}$72 was effective in creating several changes from N[25] to
NA[26]. Some of the important ones are as follows: 1 Peter 1:22;
5:2; 2 Peter 2:4, 20 (see the critical apparatus of NA[26] and my
1990 book for discussions on these passages). And yet there are
a few other readings that I would include in the text that were
rejected by the editors of NA[26] (see 1 Pet. 3:18 and 2 Pet. 1:3 in
chap. 10).

$\mathfrak{P}$75 (Bodmer Papyrus XIV–XV), ca. 175

Unquestionably, $\mathfrak{P}$75 is the best extant copy of any substantial portion of the New Testament. $\mathfrak{P}$75 contains large portions
of Luke and John. The photographs and complete transcription
of the text were first published by Victor Martin and Rudolphe
Kasser in 1961. $\mathfrak{P}$75 is the work of a professional scribe—a
scribe who very likely labored in a scriptorium in Alexandria
or in another scriptorium influenced by Alexandrian scriptoral
practices.

$\mathfrak{P}$75 displays the penmanship of a professional. According to
Martin (Martin and Kasser 1961: 1.13), "The writing is an
attractive vertical uncial—elegant and well-crafted, of the type

---

1. According to Birdsall 1971: 336, $\mathfrak{P}$72 attests some readings in Jude
unknown to later Greek traditions, but found in Clement of Alexandria and in
Latin, Sahidic, and Syriac versions.

represented by the Oxyrhynchus Papyri 2293, 2322, 2362, 2363, 2370." The handwriting displayed in these Oxyrhynchus papyri is typically called by paleographers "the common angular type of the late second to early third century."[2]

The papyrus used in $\mathfrak{P}$75 is of very fine quality—such that the verso is generally as smooth as the recto. The codex originally consisted of seventy-two leaves (144 pages) and contained only Luke and John. The outermost leaves and two innermost folios did not survive, leaving a codex that preserves Luke 3:18–4:2; 4:34–5:10; 5:37–18:18; 22:4–24:53; John 1:1–11:45; 11:48–57; 12:3–13:1; 13:8–9; 14:8–30; 15:7–8. The large typeface of the text indicates that the manuscript was composed to be read aloud to a Christian congregation. The scribe made a few corrections, and he used a system of sectional divisions that resembles that of $\mathfrak{P}$64/67 and reappears in $\aleph$ and B. The construction of this almost completely intact manuscript reveals that the scribe did not use pagination. For such a large manuscript to be assembled without the aid of pagination indicates that the scribe was quite accomplished and also very dependent on his exemplar. Of course, it is possible that the 144-page manuscript was first stitched together—before the scribe even began to copy his text—which would have aided him in keeping the proper order.

Some time after its original production, a leather cover was put around the codex to reinforce its binding. Through the centuries, the outermost pages of the codex deteriorated and those that were left in the outermost positions adhered to the cover. Inside the leather cover was found a fragment written in Coptic.

$\mathfrak{P}$75 was originally written on thirty-six folios (4 pages per folio yields 144 pages total). The outer six folios are not extant and the next outermost four folios have large gaps. In other words, the outermost ten folios (20 pages at the beginning and 20 pages at the end) are not complete. According to Martin, the original intact manuscript must have included all of Luke and all of John—up to John 21:25. But there is every indication that $\mathfrak{P}$75 originally contained only twenty chapters in John, mak-

---

2. The editors of *The Oxyrhnychus Papyri* have dated these papyri to the second and early third centuries. All of them exhibit the common angular hand. The same scribe did both 2362 and 2363 in a finely executed hand.

ing it the earliest extant copy of the first edition of John's Gospel (see the appendix for a full discussion on this).

𝔓75 has been regarded as an extremely accurate copy. Now it could be regarded as an extremely accurate copy of the first edition of John's Gospel. Many New Testament scholars agree that the Gospel of John was produced in at least two editions: one with twenty chapters and a second with an appended chapter (the twenty-first). However, the scholars who advocate this have not provided any textual evidence to verify the existence of two editions. Thus, their suppositions have been based on internal literary evidence—as opposed to external textual evidence. 𝔓75 provides the textual evidence (as does 𝔓5, most likely).

If, in fact, 𝔓75 gives witness to a first-edition copy of the Gospel of John, we would have to consider an earlier date for this manuscript than is generally given. Martin (Martin and Kasser 1961: 1.13) dates 𝔓75 in the Imperial era of 175 to 225. In a recent study (1989), Barbara Aland dates the manuscript closer to 175. I agree with this date—and urge that it is probably near 175.

As has been repeatedly mentioned in this book, 𝔓75 is eminently recognized as an extremely accurate copy. Concerning the scribe who made 𝔓75, Colwell (1965: 386, 381; repr. pp. 121, 117) writes that his "impulse to improve style is for the most part defeated by the obligation to make an exact copy"; "in 𝔓75 the text that is produced can be explained in all its variants as the result of a single force, namely the disciplined scribe who writes with the intention of being careful and accurate." All in all, 𝔓75 is a thorough literary production of the highest quality. This carefully made manuscript is an excellent copy of the original text.

It should not surprise us that another accurate manuscript, Codex Vaticanus (B), is quite close to 𝔓75. The scribe of B used either 𝔓75 itself for the Gospels of Luke and John or a manuscript quite like it. When the scribe of B (who very likely worked in Alexandria) made his complete New Testament text in one codex, he used manuscripts like 𝔓75 for Luke and John, 𝔓46 for the Pauline Epistles, and 𝔓72 for 1–2 Peter.

Studies have shown a high percentage of agreement between 𝔓75 and B. In John, Porter (1962) demonstrates 87% agreement and Edwards (1974: 71) 92% agreement (with 96% agreement in chap. 12).[3] Edwards also points out that $\mathfrak{P}$75 and B have thirty-five significant readings in John common only to themselves, as well as some common idiosyncrasies—such as the misspelling σχίμα for σχίσμα in John 7:43. Some of their paired readings likely preserve the original text (e.g., John 4:11, 42, 52; 5:2, 19; 7:42; 11:17—see the discussions in Edwards 1974: 99ff.). In the Gospel of John, $\mathfrak{P}$75 and B preserve most of the original wording of the text. When B diverges from $\mathfrak{P}$75, it is usually the result of scribal error. Seldom do we see the scribe of B adopting a variant reading from a different tradition. This speaks of the excellent testimony of $\mathfrak{P}$75 (and its successive copies). Aside from some obvious scribal errors, the testimony of $\mathfrak{P}$75 should be followed meticulously. Not surprisingly, the editors of NA[26] followed $\mathfrak{P}$75's witness 87% of the time. And it is quite noticeable that $\mathfrak{P}$75 had a tremendous impact on changes that were made from N[25] to NA[26]. For example, the testimony of $\mathfrak{P}$75 supporting the various additions in Luke 24:36, 40, 51, 52 added enough extra weight to override Westcott and Hort's "Western noninterpolations" in the last chapter of Luke. However, the testimony of $\mathfrak{P}$75 with respect to certain omissions of text should be accepted in the following passages: Luke 22:43–44; 23:34; John 9:38 (see discussions of these verses in chap. 10).

3. Edwards checked 2,199 variant readings, using $\mathfrak{P}$75 as the basic text for collation.

Chapter Eight

TEXTUAL RELATIONSHIPS AMONG THE EARLY MANUSCRIPTS: A BOOK-BY-BOOK ANALYSIS

In the preceding chapters I have made a close and thorough examination of the most significant early manuscripts. However, I have not yet attempted to formulate textual relationships among the various manuscripts or to reconstruct the history of the early transmission of the text based upon the evidence of the early manuscripts. This is a difficult—if not impossible—task to do for the entire New Testament; however, it is not as difficult to do for books or smaller portions of the New Testament because each book or portion has had its own textual history.

One textual scholar, Eldon Epp, has made some very creative attempts at reconstructing a manuscript tradition. Epp suggests that we look upon the history of the textual transmission of the New Testament from the early papyri to later manuscripts as forming trajectories or textual streams. He sees one line (called Alexandrian or Neutral—the latter being the designation given by Westcott and Hort to Codex B and then to ℵ) as "plotted first from $\mathfrak{P}$75, then perhaps through $\mathfrak{P}$23, $\mathfrak{P}$20, 0220, $\mathfrak{P}$50, etc., to Codex B and thence on through the centuries, e.g., to Codex L (8th century), manuscripts 33 (9th century), 1739 (10th century), and 579 (13th century)" (Epp 1974: 397–98). He sees another line (called Western or D-type) as moving from "$\mathfrak{P}$5 and $\mathfrak{P}$29 through $\mathfrak{P}$48, $\mathfrak{P}$38, $\mathfrak{P}$37, and 0171, then to codices D and D_p, and thence on through the centuries to F_p and G_p (9th century) and manuscripts 614 and 383 (13th century)" (Epp 1974: 398). Several other papyri (such as $\mathfrak{P}$46 and $\mathfrak{P}$66), Epp says, stand midway between the aforementioned trajectories and do not develop textual streams of their own—with the exception of $\mathfrak{P}$45, which leads abortively to Codex W. Epp believes (1980: 148) that "with admitted caution, these lines of trajectory also may be extended *backwards* behind (i.e., earlier than) the earliest papyri and uncials to show presumed lines of development."

Epp's trajectories are intriguing but could be misleading because such trajectories cannot be applied to the whole New Testament text. Rather, trajectories have to be drawn on a book-by-book basis because each book (or group of books) of the New Testament has had its own textual history. For example, the Western trajectory proposed by Epp works only for the Book of Acts. $\mathfrak{P}$29, $\mathfrak{P}$48, and $\mathfrak{P}$38 can be applied only to the Book of Acts; there are no other early papyri with a D-type text. 0171, an early uncial manuscript, is a D-type text for Matthew and Luke. ($\mathfrak{P}$5, containing John, is more closely related to $\aleph$ than D; and $\mathfrak{P}$37 is closer to $\mathfrak{P}$45 than to D.) Furthermore, another trajectory can be drawn for another kind of text of the Book of Acts. This begins with $\mathfrak{P}$91 (and perhaps $\mathfrak{P}$45)[1] and goes on to B, $\aleph$, $\mathfrak{P}$50, A, C, $\mathfrak{P}$74, 33, 81, 104, 326, and 1175. Thus, for the Book of Acts, there were two text types that existed as early as the second century. Many scholars believe that the D-type text was not the work of the original author, Luke, but the work of a "reviser, who was obviously a meticulous and well-informed scholar, [who] eliminated seams and gaps and added historical, biographical, and geographical details. Apparently, the reviser did his work at an early date, before the text of Acts had come to be generally regarded as a sacred text that must be

---

1. $\mathfrak{P}$45, the earliest papyrus containing Acts, agrees with $\aleph$ (63%) and B (62%); whereas its agreement with D is far less (54%).

preserved inviolate" (Metzger 1971: 270). The text of Acts circulated in two forms; the earliest form is that which is preserved in 𝔓45, 𝔓91, 0189, ℵ, B, 𝔓53, 𝔓50, and 𝔓74.

In a more recent essay (1989a), Epp clarifies his concept of the trajectories with respect to the book-by-book nature of text-typing. He argues for the existence of three different text types in the second century: B (for manuscripts like 𝔓75 and B), C (for the so-called Caesarean manuscripts like 𝔓45), and D (for the D-type manuscripts such as 𝔓29, 𝔓38, 𝔓48, and 0171). (The A category stands for Koine/Byzantine-type manuscripts such as A [in the Gospels], but all such manuscripts are fifth century or later.) In categorizing the early manuscripts in these groups, the D category is troublesome because it attempts to encompass both D-type manuscripts and so-called Western manuscripts. D-type manuscripts (i.e., manuscripts related to Codex Bezae) are classifiable, but not Western manuscripts, for there is really no such text type as a Western text. The Western text is the popular text of the late second or early third century.

Concerning the early manuscripts, the C-type text is really found only in 𝔓45 (for Mark) and perhaps 𝔓37 (for Matthew)—which shows agreement with 𝔓45. (𝔓37 aligns with 𝔓45 all eight times where there is textual variation in the verses they have in common: Matt. 26:20–38.) 𝔓27 and 𝔓35 do not belong in this category, for both show marked agreement with B and ℵ. 𝔓8, listed by Epp, is an independent text; nevertheless, it shows agreement with B in significant variants.

The D-type text is not clearly found in any early manuscript besides those that contain the Gospels and Acts, including the following early manuscripts listed by Epp: 𝔓29, 𝔓38, 𝔓48, and 0189. All the other manuscripts listed by Epp are questionable (indeed he places a question mark next to several of his citations). For example, 𝔓5 has far greater affinity with ℵ than with D, and 𝔓72 (in Jude) is merely an independent text. 𝔓69 is the only other early manuscript that resembles a D-type text, but it too is an independent text, "similar but unrelated to D" (Aland and Aland 1987: 100). 𝔓69 has three examples of characteristic D-type readings, counterbalanced by eight disagreements with D. Thus, we cannot produce a trajectory for any book of the New Testament (besides the Gospels and Acts) that begins with an early papyrus (or uncial) and leads to D. However, a trajectory can be drawn for many other books beginning with the papyri and leading to later manuscripts, especially ℵ and B.

In Matthew, 𝔓1, 𝔓35, and 𝔓71 lead to B, while 𝔓64/67 and 𝔓77 show agreement with ℵ. 0171 is D-type text, and 𝔓37 and 𝔓45 have great affinity. In Mark, 𝔓45 agrees with W (70%). In Luke, 𝔓4 and B are in agreement—in fact, 𝔓4 concurs with B as against ℵ. In both Luke and John 𝔓75 is a precursor to B (with 83% agreement). In John, several papyri show marked affinities with ℵ: 𝔓22, 𝔓66, 𝔓90 (in chaps. 6–7), and 𝔓5 (but less than the others). 𝔓39 and B are in complete agreement. In Acts, 𝔓29, 𝔓38 (especially), and 𝔓48 show agreement with D, while 𝔓45, 𝔓53, and 𝔓91 show agreement with ℵ and B. In the Pauline Epistles 𝔓46 is a precursor to B (with 75%–80% agreement) and to 1739. 𝔓27, 𝔓49, and 0220 also display closeness to B, while 𝔓40, 𝔓65, and 𝔓92 have affinities with 𝔓46, ℵ, and B. In Titus, 𝔓32 agrees with ℵ, F, and G. In Hebrews 𝔓46 is very closely related to 𝔓13 (with 80% agreement) and B (with 79% agreement). In James 𝔓20 is aligned with B (then ℵ and C), while 𝔓23 is aligned with ℵ, B, and C. In 1 Peter 𝔓72 shows the greatest agreement with B, then A; whereas 𝔓81 is in agreement with B, then 𝔓72. In 2 Peter 𝔓72 has some agreement with B. In Revelation 𝔓47 has general agreement with ℵ, C, P, and A. And 𝔓85 is in full agreement with 𝔓47 and ℵ. 𝔓18 shows agreement with A, C, and ℵ (in that order).

We can imagine that each of these papyri had an ancestor in its line. For most books, that ancestor was definitely a proto-ℵ/B-type text. And since we are fairly certain that there were not any late first-century or early second-century recensions (with the exception of Acts), it is safe to assume that the original text looked like ℵ and B in most books, except in a purer form—or, should I say, the purest form. This tells us that the Alexandrian scribes faithfully transmitted the original text (with minor editorial revisions). It is no wonder, then, that Kenyon (1951: 116) says that ℵ and B are modeled after the best examples of the second-century papyrus. And it is also no wonder that most scholars believe that both ℵ and B were produced in the Alexandrian scriptorium. Scribe A of Codex Vaticanus was the same scribe as scribe D of Codex Sinaiticus (Milne and Skeat 1938: 89–90). Furthermore, the order of books in both manuscripts is identical with that found in the statement made by Bishop Athanasius of Alexandria about the canon of Scripture.[2]

The reviser of Acts produced an early textual form that persisted for generations, and the scribe of 𝔓45 (given his proclivities for creative independence) seems to be the perpetrator of a new text type for Mark that led to W.[3] All the rest of the papyri generally affirm an א- or B-type text (the product of Alexandrian scriptoral practices) or a popular type text (sometimes called Western), which is the kind of text that contains a normal amount of errors and scribal emendations—and does not display any marked uniformity (except that it is different from the proto-Alexandrian text). Generally speaking, the original text is not likely to be found in readings supported exclusively by C-type texts or D-type texts. The original text is more likely to be found in the B-type texts, which show specific and/or general agreement with the two great uncials, א and B. Quite specifically, one could say that manuscripts like 𝔓4/64/67, 𝔓46, and 𝔓75 are the most accurate copies of the original text.

The following diagrams and accompanying text attempt to portray the early textual history of each book or section of the New Testament. Each diagram gives dates and manuscript relationships—both to the original and (often) to other manuscripts. Manuscripts appearing in the center of the diagram are closer to the original—the earlier the better. Manuscripts further from the middle are further from the original, regardless of date. (Of course, original readings can and have been preserved in these manuscripts, but the diagrams depict their general disposition.) Manuscripts placed left of center tend to resemble the Western text, the D-type text, or an independent text. Manuscripts placed right of center tend to resemble the Byzantine text. Those in the center are usually Alexandrian or proto-Alexandrian.

2. However, the pagination of B "reveals that *Vaticanus* was based on an early copy in which Hebrews came between Galatians and Ephesians. In that earlier copy Galatians began with chapter 54 [in an ancient system of numbering Paul's epistles continuously] and ended with chapter 59, but Ephesians began with chapter 70. These chapter numberings were taken over unchanged by *Vaticanus*, in which Hebrews, although its position has been changed, begins with chapter 60 and presumably ended with chapter 69" (Bruce 1988: 206).

3. One could also say that 𝔓45 led to a 𝔓37-type text (or C-type text) in Matthew, but the portion common to both papyri (Matt. 26:20–38) is too small to make a definite statement about the textual relationship of 𝔓45 and 𝔓37.

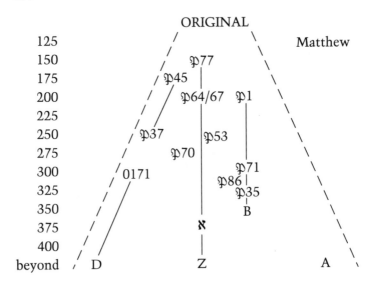

Matthew

After Matthew wrote and published his Gospel (perhaps in Antioch), it received immediate and universal recognition as being the first Gospel. Matthew's popularity is manifest in the fact that this Gospel is extant in the second largest number of early manuscripts (John is first). Among these manuscripts are some very important documents. The earliest copy is 𝔓77 (ca. 150), the work of a professional scribe who worked in an Oxyrhynchian scriptorium and was well acquainted with producing literary texts. The next earliest manuscript is 𝔓1, the first Oxyrhynchian New Testament manuscript. This, also, is a copy made by a trained scribe working around 200. Another early copy is found in the manuscript 𝔓64/67 (ca. 200), a thoroughgoing literary work produced by a trained scribe. Other early Matthean manuscripts are 𝔓45 (150–175) and 𝔓37 (ca. 250), which bear remarkable resemblance—thereby revealing that the scribe of 𝔓37 worked from a manuscript much like 𝔓45.

Quite interestingly, three strands of textual affinities can be seen in the early development of Matthew: (1) 𝔓1—𝔓71—𝔓35—B; (2) 𝔓77—𝔓64/67—ℵ; (3) 𝔓45—𝔓37. All three strands are similar to one another and could be called Alexandrian. The D-type is evident in 0171 and D. The original text can usually be found in the first two groups, if not in the third. A reading is especially likely to be original if it is supported by manuscripts from the three clusters.

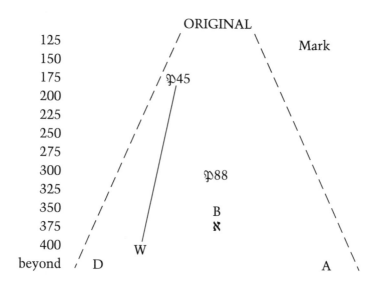

Mark

Ironically, the earliest Gospel, Mark (written 65–70), has not been preserved in very many early manuscripts. And to add to the irony (and mystery), Mark was supposed to have taken his Gospel with him to Egypt (Eusebius, *Ecclesiastical History* 2:16:1)—and yet there are hardly any early extant copies of Mark among the many discoveries of manuscripts in Egypt. The earliest copy of Mark is preserved in 𝔓45, but it is not a very faithful copy. In the Book of Mark especially, the scribe of 𝔓45 exerted many personal liberties in making a text that replicated more the *thought* of his exemplar than the actual words. As is well known, 𝔓45 has marked affinities with the fifth-century manuscript W. The more "normal" text of Mark is preserved in one early fourth-century manuscript, 𝔓88, and two later fourth-century manuscripts, ℵ and B. Until there are more discoveries of early Marcan manuscripts, it is difficult to reconstruct the early history of the text.

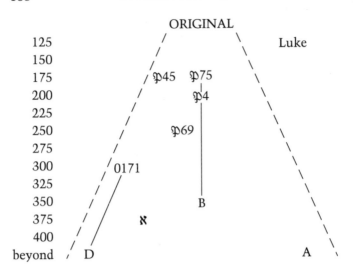

Luke

Luke composed his Gospel (and the Book of Acts) under the literary patronage of Theophilus, in accordance with the custom of the times. Very likely, the original copy was given to Theophilus, and Luke kept a copy or two for himself. Theophilus, functioning as the publisher (see Goodspeed 1954), had the archetypal text, from which other copies would be made for distribution in the book trade and for deposition in Rome's library. The literary quality of these books and their intended purpose (i.e., to reach "god-fearers" and to make Christianity a *religio licita*) would call for a secular distribution. And, quite particularly, Luke may have wanted the Roman officials to read his works. (Theophilus, called "most excellent"—a title given to the Roman governors Felix and Festus [Acts 23:26; 24:3; 26:25]—could have been a Roman official.) Of course, copies would have also been made for several Pauline churches, to whom Luke was a well-known and respected leader.

The Gospel of Luke has been preserved in several early manuscripts. 𝔓45 contains large portions of Luke, and 𝔓75 preserves Luke 4–24. Luke's original wording is best preserved in 𝔓4 (the work of a trained scribe and part of the same manuscript as 𝔓64/67) and 𝔓75. Quite significantly, both 𝔓4 and 𝔓75 lead to a B-type text. The original text is largely retained in 𝔓4,

𝔓75, and B. The testimony of 𝔓45 adds weight. As in Matthew, 0171 concurs with D.

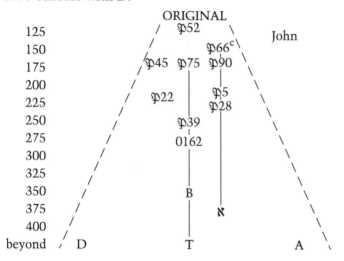

John

The first copies of John were circulated to the churches throughout Asia Minor and beyond at the end of the first century. The first edition may have included only twenty chapters, which was then quickly replaced by the second and final edition, including the appended, twenty-first chapter. This Gospel was widely circulated shortly after the time of its publication.

One of the earliest copies to be made in Egypt was 𝔓52 (dated around 110), a manuscript that could have originated in Alexandria and then been taken to the Fayum or Oxyrhynchus. Although it is just a scrap, paleographers have been able to determine that it was part of an entire codex. This manuscript, had it been preserved complete, would have given us a second- or third-generation copy of the original text!

Around the middle of the second century in a scriptorium in Egypt, a novice scribe prepared a copy of John's Gospel. He was a wonderful calligrapher but a not-so-wonderful copyist. Under the direction of a *diorthōtēs* (corrector), he made several corrections in his manuscript. Some of these corrections were made from his original exemplar and others from another exemplar (it was not uncommon in antiquity for scribes to check a work of literature against a different examplar and then make a collated, corrected copy). This manuscript, known as 𝔓66, was a third- or fourth-generation manuscript, preserving (after corrections) much of the original text but also introducing some textual corruptions into the text.

A generation later, around 175, another scribe working in an Egyptian scriptorium (perhaps the same one in which the scribe of 𝔓66 worked, for both manuscripts were found in the same library) had access to a very accurate copy of Luke and John and then produced another accurate replica that preserves most of the original wording of Luke and John. This manuscript, known as 𝔓75, is the best specimen of scribal acumen.

Around the same time, Christian scribes in Oxyrhynchus were preparing manuscripts for the churches in that city. 𝔓90, prepared around 175, preserves John 18–19 in a text somewhat similar to 𝔓66. Other manuscripts containing portions of John have been discovered in Oxyrhynchus, many of which date in the early third century. Of note are 𝔓5 and 𝔓22, which have marked disagreements in John 16. Another noteworthy manuscript is 𝔓39, because it shows remarkable agreement with 𝔓75.

After 150 years, in the middle of the fourth century, certain Alexandrian scribes prepared codexes of the entire New Testament. When the scribe of B prepared Luke and John, he used a manuscript very similar to 𝔓75 (as well as 𝔓39 and 0162). When the scribe of ℵ prepared John, he used a manuscript (or manuscripts) that had more similarities with 𝔓5, 𝔓66ᶜ, and 𝔓90.

The Gospel of John, above all other New Testament books, possesses the greatest number of papyrus manuscripts dated before 250–300. Twelve in total (𝔓5, 𝔓6, 𝔓22, 𝔓28, 𝔓39, 𝔓45, 𝔓52, 𝔓66, 𝔓75, 𝔓80, 𝔓90, and 𝔓95), these manuscripts provide a good base for recovering the original text of John. They are not monolithic in their text; there are definite differences in text types, not necessarily in the larger sense of Alexandrian, Western, etc., but in a more limited sense of associations among themselves and with other later manuscripts. Three of the manuscripts are too fragmentary to determine their textual affinities: 𝔓52, 𝔓80, and 𝔓95. The other manuscripts can be placed in three categories: (1) those that show affinity with B: 𝔓6 (in part), 𝔓28, 𝔓39, and especially 𝔓75; (2) those that show affinity with ℵ: 𝔓5, 𝔓66, and 𝔓90; and (3) those that show obvious independence: 𝔓22 and 𝔓45.

It is well known that 𝔓75 was a precursor to B—or, at least, one could say that the scribe of B used a manuscript very much like 𝔓75 as his exemplar. Only one other early manuscript shows the same likeness: 𝔓39. It is less well known but equally true that 𝔓66 has many similarities to ℵ, especially from 8:39 to the end of the book. ℵ is clearly a Western text in 1:1–8:38 (Fee 1968). In this same section, however, 𝔓66 is closer to C, B, A, and 𝔓75 (in that order). (𝔓66ᶜ is very close to C and 𝔓75 and thereby reveals that the corrector of 𝔓66 probably used an exemplar like a precursor to C or 𝔓75.) In several significant variation units, 𝔓5 has the same reading as ℵ. And 𝔓90 exhibits greater resemblance to ℵ than to B. Even 𝔓22 and 𝔓45, though independent, are closer to ℵ than to B. These groupings show that various textual streams were developing at a very early date—but the three predominant streams are the ones leading to a B-type text, an ℵ-type text, and a C-type text. Among the early Johannine papyri there are no manuscripts that clearly antedate a D-type text.

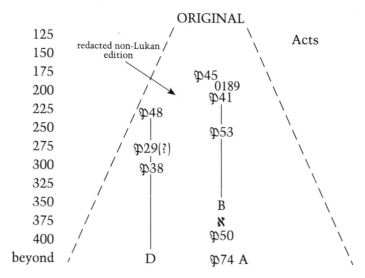

Acts

The Book of Acts was published as a sequel to Luke's Gospel; it also was written under the patronage of Theophilus. It is possible that Theophilus was a Christian lawyer who was called upon to defend Paul in his Roman trial, in which case the Book of Acts would have served as a historical defense of the legitimacy of Christianity. Some scholars have argued that Luke published a second, revised and expanded edition of Acts shortly after the first edition was released. But it seems more likely that the expanded edition was the work of a second-century reviser.

There is extant evidence for the revised form of Acts beginning in the third century. 𝔓48, 𝔓38, and perhaps 𝔓29 are precursors to the form of the text found in D (having the most complete presentation of the expanded form of Acts). However, the first edition has earlier evidence—in the manuscripts 𝔓45, 0189, and 𝔓91. These manuscripts, basically Alexandrian in character, represent the kinds of manuscripts that the copyists of 𝔓53, B, ℵ, 𝔓50, A, and 𝔓74 used in making their copies of Acts. The original text is basically preserved by their testimony.

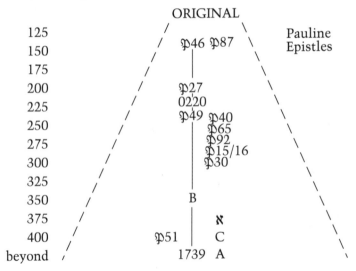

	ORIGINAL	
125	/ \	Pauline
150	/ 𝔓46 𝔓87 \	Epistles
175	/ \	
200	/ 𝔓27 \	
225	/ 0220 \	
250	/ 𝔓49 𝔓40 \	
275	/ 𝔓65 \	
	/ 𝔓92 \	
300	/ 𝔓15/16 \	
	/ 𝔓30 \	
325	/ \	
350	/ B \	
375	/ ℵ \	
400	/ 𝔓51 C \	
beyond	/ 1739 A \	

Pauline Epistles (Excluding Pastoral Epistles)

Paul's epistles were originally sent to the various churches under his ministry: Rome, Corinth, Thessalonica, Philippi, churches in Galatia, and churches in Asia Minor (including Ephesus and Colossae). These churches would have kept the original manuscript, from which copies would be made for other nearby churches (see Col. 4:16). Paul, or perhaps his amanuensis, very likely kept copies of his own epistles.

It is likely that someone in Paul's circle, after Paul's death, collected his epistles into one corpus, which would include Romans, 1–2 Corinthians, Galatians, Ephesians, Philippians, Colossians, 1–2 Thessalonians, Philemon, and perhaps Hebrews—but not the pastoral Epistles (see the next section). The collector or compiler could have been Luke or Timothy. C. F. D. Moule (1962: 204) argues for Luke, saying, "It is entirely in keeping with his historian's temperament to collect them." The collector could have also taken on the role of a compiling editor whose task was to gather all the Pauline documents into one corpus. For example, this compiler could have added a final chapter to Romans (chap. 16) and connected Paul's third epistle to the Corinthians (2 Cor. 10–13) to the fourth (2 Cor. 1–9). But it is very unlikely that the compiler would have changed Paul's original wording because the original, individual manuscripts (or early copies thereof) would have still been in existence and would have thereby exposed an emended text as being fraudulent.

Several early manuscripts have been discovered that originally contained the Pauline corpus. The most celebrated is 𝔓46 because of its date and because it preserves nearly all of the Pauline Epistles. If Kim's dating (1988) of 𝔓46 is accepted (or even adjusted upward by fifty years), this manuscript dates anywhere between 85 and 150. If the date is 85, 𝔓46 is a first- or second-generation copy of the Pauline corpus. At the most, it is a fourth- or fifth-generation copy. 𝔓46 was a professionally made copy produced in a scriptorium in Alexandria or some other Egyptian city. Aside from noticeable scribal blunders (that were left uncorrected), it largely preserves the original text.

A few other early manuscripts give evidence of a Pauline corpus. 𝔓15 and 𝔓16, parts of the same manuscript, preserve portions of 1 Corinthians and Philippians. The complete manuscript must have included the entire Pauline corpus. 𝔓92 retains portions of Ephesians and 1 Thessalonians. The pagination of 𝔓13 reveals that the complete manuscript of this work originally contained Romans just prior to Hebrews.

The fourth-century manuscript B must have been copied from a manuscript much like 𝔓46 (and 𝔓13). When the Western tendencies of B (noted by its alignment with D and F/G) are eliminated, the testimony of 𝔓46 and B often represents the original text. The other fourth-century manuscript, א, was also copied from a manuscript very much like 𝔓46—as well as from manuscripts like 𝔓13, 𝔓15/16, 𝔓40, and 0220. The original text has largely been preserved in any combination of these manuscripts—especially when there are three or more giving testimony.

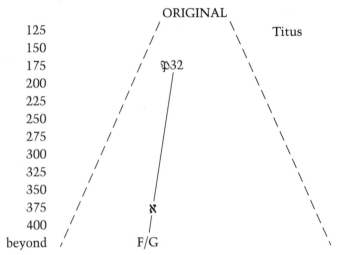

Pastoral Epistles

The pastoral Epistles have a different history than the other Pauline Epistles because they were private letters to individuals that would not have been intended for circulation among the churches. Gradually, the pastoral Epistles gained recognition and acceptance into the Pauline canon. (The Epistle to Philemon, although also a personal letter, gained immediate recognition because of its connection with Colossians.) There is only one early copy of one pastoral epistle, 𝔓32, displaying part of Titus (chap. 2). The work of a professional scribe around 175, this papyrus (which cannot be compared with B because Vaticanus lacks the pastoral Epistles) shows affinity with א and F/G.

Hebrews

Hebrews was included in the Pauline corpus according to 𝔓46 and (very likely) 𝔓13. Another early manuscript containing a portion of Hebrews is 𝔓17. The copyist of 𝔓13 used a manu-

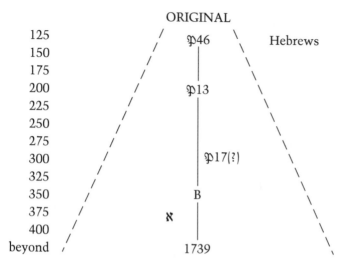

script very much like 𝔓46, and the copyist of B used an exemplar very much like 𝔓46 and 𝔓13. The original text of Hebrews has been largely preserved in 𝔓13, 𝔓46, and B.

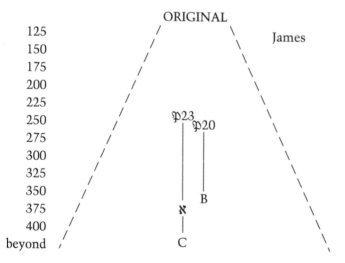

James

There are two extant third-century manuscripts of James: 𝔓23 showing affinities with ℵ and C, and 𝔓20 bearing resemblance to B. These manuscripts usually reflect the original wording of the text.

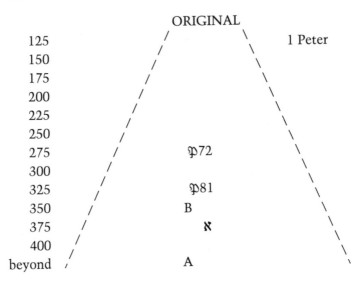

1 Peter

Peter's first epistle, accepted from the onset as authentic and apostolic, was quite well preserved in its early textual transmission. This textual fidelity is manifest in one late third-century manuscript, 𝔓72, and another fourth-century manuscript, 𝔓81. 𝔓72 displays a text that resembles B and yet is closer to the original than B, while 𝔓81 has more affinity with א than with B.

2 Peter and Jude

The original text of 2 Peter and Jude was not as well preserved in the early period of textual transmission because these books were not readily acknowledged as apostolic, canonical texts by all sectors of the early church. The manuscript evidence for these books is quite diverse and marked by independence. This is evident in the two papyri, 𝔓72 (especially for Jude) and 𝔓78.

1–3 John

Unlike John's Gospel, which was very popular throughout the early church, John's epistles were far less known and read. A portion of 1 John exists in one third-century papyrus, 𝔓9 (a

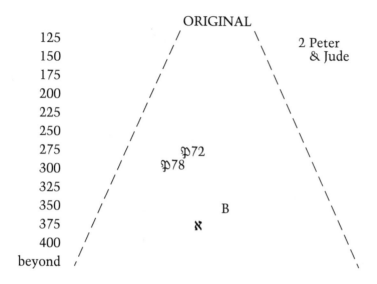

product of careless copying), and a portion of 2 John exists in one fourth-century vellum manuscript, 0232 (which could have originally contained the entire Johannine corpus: Gospel, Epistles, Revelation). Out of all the manuscripts, 0232 bears the most resemblance to A.

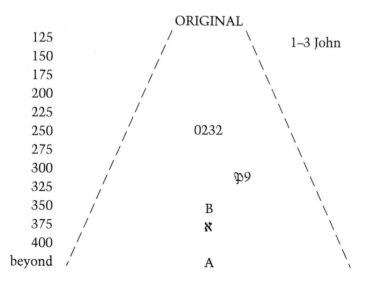

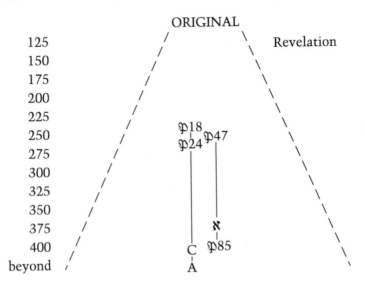

Revelation

Although the early textual history of Revelation is not as clear as one would like it to be, it is apparent that some scribes (generation after generation) treated the text carefully. According to Joseph Schmid (who produced a magnum opus on the text of Revelation in 1955–56), the best text was preserved in A and C. This text seems to have been antedated by the two third-century manuscripts, 𝔓18 and 𝔓24. The second best text is that found in ℵ, whose precursor is 𝔓47. The original reading is usually found in either stream: 𝔓18—𝔓24—A—C or 𝔓47—𝔓85—ℵ.

Chapter Nine

The Early Text Compared to the Nestle–Aland Text (NA²⁶)

A ccording to the evidence we now have, the early period of textual transmission (from the late first century to the early fourth century) displayed both freedom and fidelity. Manuscripts were produced with varying degrees of accuracy. Origen is often quoted in this regard (*Commentary on St. Matthew* 15:14):

> Nowadays, as is evident, there is a great diversity between the various manuscripts, either through the negligence of certain copyists, or the perverse audacity shown by some in correcting the text, or through the fault of those who, playing the part of correctors, lengthen or shorten it as they please.

But this quotation, cited so often in books about New Testament textual criticism, has to be understood in its context. Origen was making a complaint about the diversity of manuscripts in the Synoptic Gospels concerning a disharmony of wording between Matthew 19:19 (the verse he was commenting on) and Mark 10:19 and Luke 18:20. Because Mark and Luke do not have the statement *Love your neighbor as your-*

119

self, while Matthew does, Origen blamed the discrepancy on textual corruption. However, among all the extant manuscripts there is no evidence of textual corruption in any of these passages. Origen, like many modern harmonists, was trying to blame scribal tampering for the lack of harmony among the Gospels.

After Origen made this complaint about textual variation among the Gospels, he went on to explain how he had labored to produce an Old Testament text that dealt with the discrepancies between the Septuagint and the Hebrew text. Yet he was very honest in saying, "I do not think I could do the same on New Testament texts without danger." Thus, Origen occupied himself (and most of the catechetical schools at Alexandria and Caesarea) with the Hexapla project, wherein he spent his energies correcting the Old Testament text. Origen said (*Opera Omina* 17:5), "The work of correction leaves us no time for supper, for exercise, or for rest. Even at these times we are compelled to study and to emend manuscripts." He recognized the need to emend the New Testament text and on occasion spoke of specific passages, but he never produced an emended New Testament text. Nor did Demetrius, the bishop of Alexandria in Origen's day, because the energies of the catechetical school were directed toward producing an accurate Old Testament text for their apologetics.

During the second century, there were a few men who produced recensions of the New Testament text. According to Eusebius, Theodotus (and his followers) altered the text for their own purposes. In the middle of the second century, Marcion "expunged his copies of the Gospel according to Luke of all references to the Jewish background of Jesus," and "Tatian's Harmony of the Gospels contains several textual alterations which lent support to ascetic and encratic views" (Metzger 1968: 201). And yet another recensionist created the D-type text for the Gospels and Acts. This theologically minded redactor, living in the late second or third century, created a text that had short-lived popularity. Three third-century papyri, $\mathfrak{P}$29, $\mathfrak{P}$38, and $\mathfrak{P}$48, each containing a portion from the Book of Acts, are precursors to the D-type text in Acts. But there are other papyri containing portions of Acts that provide even earlier testimony to a purer form of Acts—namely, $\mathfrak{P}$45 (ca. 150) and $\mathfrak{P}$91 (ca.

200)—thereby showing that the D text of Acts did not necessarily antedate the purer form (see discussion in chap. 8).

Besides these endeavors—which are all noted for creating textual impurities—there was no recension of the New Testament text in the second century. Rather, this was a period in which some scribes exercised freedom in copying and some demonstrated acumen. The manuscripts produced by the latter are those that come closest to preserving the original text. A prime example of an accurate late second-century manuscript is 𝔓75.

It is a well-known fact that the text produced by the scribe of 𝔓75 is a very accurate manuscript. It is also well known that 𝔓75 was the kind of manuscript used in formulating Codex Vaticanus—the readings of 𝔓75 and B are remarkably similar (see Porter 1962). Prior to the discovery of 𝔓75, certain scholars thought Codex Vaticanus was the work of a fourth-century recension; others (chiefly Hort) thought it must trace back to a very early and accurate copy. Hort said that Codex Vaticanus preserves "not only a very ancient text, but a very pure line of very ancient text" (Westcott and Hort 1882: introduction pp. 250–51). 𝔓75 appears to have shown that Hort was right.

Prior to the discovery of 𝔓75, many textual scholars were convinced that the second- and third-century papyri displayed a text in flux, a text characterized only by individual independence. The Chester Beatty papyri (𝔓45) and the Bodmer papyri (𝔓66 and 𝔓72—in 2 Peter and Jude) show this kind of independence. Scholars thought that scribes at Alexandria must have used several such texts to produce a good recension—as is exhibited in Codex Vaticanus. But 𝔓75 has proven this theory wrong. What is quite clear now is that Codex Vaticanus was simply a copy (with some modifications) of a manuscript much like 𝔓75, not a fourth-century recension.

Some scholars are quick to point out that this does not automatically mean that 𝔓75 and B represent the original text. What it does mean, they say, is that we have a second-century manuscript showing great affinity with a fourth-century manuscript whose quality has been highly esteemed. Gordon Fee's 1974 study demonstrates that there was no recension of any kind in early Alexandria. He says that Hort was right about B preserving "a very pure line of very ancient text." But Hort was speaking in relationship to the original text, while Fee claims he was speaking only with regard to its text type. Fee adds

(1974: 40), "The final question is whether the ancestor(s) of $\mathfrak{P}75$ B is recensional in the sense of a revised or produced text." However, it seems that Fee has answered his own question by showing that $\mathfrak{P}75$ was not recensional and therefore must be an excellent copy of the original text.

Hort was bold enough to speak of the original text, while modern scholars tend to shy away from this concept. If an autograph of the New Testament were found today, it would very likely be labeled as an ancient manuscript that preserves a pure text type with some emendations. It is time that we speak of recovering the original text—a recovery that must be based on documentary evidence and on the intrinsic value of each document; it cannot be based on a theoretical reconstruction of the early textual history. For example, we cannot explain how a D-type text coexisted with a $\mathfrak{P}75$/B-type text in the second century. All we know is that the D-type text appears to be a short-lived aberration, while the $\mathfrak{P}75$/B-type text appears to be a faithful transmission of the original text.

Of course, this kind of judgment troubles certain scholars, who point out that the esteem given to B and $\mathfrak{P}75$ is based on a subjective appreciation of the kind of text they contain (as over against the D-type text), rather than on any kind of theoretical reconstruction of the early transmission of the text (see Epp 1974: 390–93). This same subjective estimation was at work when Hort decided that B was intrinsically superior to D (Westcott and Hort 1882: introduction pp. 32–42). Yet the praxis of textual criticism time and again demonstrates that the $\mathfrak{P}75$/B-type text is intrinsically superior to the D-type text.

Kurt Aland held the view (1965: 336) that the early period of transmission was characteristically erratic and free until he realized the textual fidelity of $\mathfrak{P}75$. Aland still believes that there is no way of making a genealogy of manuscripts, but there is a way to intuitively recognize good copies—that is, those that exhibit strict adherence to an exemplar. Though there is still no way of completely knowing if this good copy is an accurate copy of an inferior text, we do know with some degree of certainty that (1) there were no organized recensions prior to the fourth century and (2) there are ways of recognizing the intrinsic quality of any given manuscript. Therefore, it is likely that an early, good (or what the Alands would call "strict") manuscript transmitted the original text quite reliably. "Early" (late

first to early third century) is important because an early manuscript has less chance of being affected than a later manuscript—even though it is true that a manuscript can be affected
at any time. Nonetheless, textual critics have to work with
what they have, and their best resource is an early manuscript
with a "strict" text.

According to the Alands (1987: 95), several of the early papyri
have a strict text: 𝔓1, 𝔓23, 𝔓27, 𝔓35, 𝔓39, 𝔓64/67, 𝔓65, 𝔓70,
and 𝔓75 (so also 0220). Others have a "normal" text (i.e., a text
transmitted with a limited amount of variation, characteristic
of the New Testament textual tradition): 𝔓4, 𝔓5, 𝔓12, 𝔓16,
𝔓18, 𝔓20, 𝔓28, 𝔓47, 𝔓52, and 𝔓87 (so also 0162, 0171, and
0189). The Alands have classified other early papyri as being
either "at least normal" or "free." Regardless of the classifica-
tion (and regardless of whether one agrees with their classifica-
tion—I disagree with 𝔓46 being called "free")—the Alands
affirm that all of the early papyri are significant for determining
the original text because of their age (1987: 93–95).

As the champion of the early papyri, Kurt Aland had the
opportunity to make great changes in the twenty-sixth edition
of the Nestle–Aland text. In all the editions prior to the twenty-
sixth, the text of the Nestle Greek New Testament was virtually the same—only the critical apparatus was revised (primarily by the addition of fresh manuscript citation). Aland,
however, desired to make a major revision of the text itself.
Aland made this revision in cooperation with four other editors (Matthew Black, Carlo Martini, Bruce Metzger, and Allen
Wikgren) who together produced the United Bible Societies'
third edition of the *Greek New Testament*. (Hence, both UBS[3]
and NA[26] share the same text, with different critical appara-
tuses.) The critical apparatus of NA[26] lists thousands of textual
variants. Of these, the early manuscripts (late first to mid-
fourth century) are cited about 2,400 times. Surprisingly, the
early papyri support the text about 1,415 times (which equals
59%). Table 1 presents the details.

What is quite apparent is that NA[26] does not fully display
the evidence of the early manuscripts. NA[26] exhibits a change
from N[25] (and all previous editions of the Nestle text) in only
176 places due to the influence of the early manuscripts. Of
course, it can be argued that the early manuscripts merely add
extra, early support to well-established readings. However,

	Changes from N[25] to NA[26]	Early manuscript readings adopted in NA[26]	Readings from individual papyri
Matthew	2	31	
Mark	5 (all due to 𝔓45)	26	
Luke	37	363	𝔓4: 29
			𝔓4 + 𝔓75: 3
			𝔓75: 280
			𝔓45 + 𝔓75: 47
			𝔓45: 4 (against 𝔓75 3 times)
John*	51	336	𝔓66: 114 (against 𝔓75 36 times)
			𝔓75: 64 (against 𝔓66 56 times)
			𝔓66 + 𝔓75: 141 (with other early MSS 15 times)
			other early MSS: 17
Acts	4	41	𝔓8: 5
			𝔓45: 31
			𝔓8 + 𝔓45: 2
			(𝔓38 was not accepted by NA[26])
Romans	15 (all due to 𝔓46)	55	𝔓46: 51
1 Corinthians	11	113	𝔓46: 107
2 Corinthians	11	86	𝔓46: 86
Galatians	2	36	𝔓46: 36
Ephesians	2	54	𝔓46: 48
			𝔓49: 1
			𝔓46 + 𝔓49: 3
			𝔓92: 1
Philippians	4	29	𝔓46: 26
			𝔓16: 1
			𝔓16 + 𝔓46: 2
Colossians	3	36	𝔓46: 36
1 Thessalonians	2	6	
Hebrews	8	77	𝔓46: 56
			𝔓13: 3
			𝔓13 + 𝔓46: 17
			𝔓17 + 𝔓46: 1
James	0	6	𝔓23: 2
			𝔓20: 4
1 Peter	9	59	𝔓72: 54
			𝔓81: 3
			𝔓72 + 𝔓81: 2
2 Peter	6	34	𝔓72: 34
Jude	3	7	𝔓72: 7
Revelation	1	20	𝔓47: 16
			𝔓18: 2
			𝔓24: 2
TOTAL	176	1,415	

*For detailed analysis of early manuscripts in the Gospel of John, see Comfort 1990b.

TABLE 1. *Use of Early Papyri in NA[26]*

NA²⁶ does not include about 980 readings that are found in the early papyri (and always supported by at least one other witness—usually many more). The number of rejections (which equals 42%) is listed as follows (the list does not include any readings supported by one manuscript alone):

Matthew	27
Mark	70 (𝔓45 was rejected 64 times)
Luke	122 (𝔓45 was rejected 63 times; 𝔓75, 40 times; 𝔓45 + 𝔓75, 9 times)
John	95 (𝔓66 was rejected 66 times; 𝔓75, 12 times; 𝔓66 + 𝔓75, 14 times)
Acts	40 (𝔓45 was rejected 23 times; 𝔓38, 7 times; 𝔓48, 4 times)
Romans	51 (all 𝔓46)
1 Corinthians	53 (all 𝔓46)
2 Corinthians	32 (all 𝔓46)
Galatians	14 (almost all 𝔓46)
Ephesians	13 (almost all 𝔓46)
Philippians	20 (almost all 𝔓46)
Colossians	5 (all 𝔓46)
1 Thessalonians	4
Titus	1
Hebrews	57 (𝔓13 was rejected 8 times; 𝔓46, 41 times; 𝔓13 + 𝔓46, 8 times)
James	2
1 Peter	37 (almost all 𝔓72)
2 Peter	8 (all 𝔓72)
Jude	11 (almost all 𝔓72)
Revelation	101 (almost all 𝔓47)

In addition to these rejections, the early papyri readings supported by B were rejected another 215 times.

Some of the rejections are defensible. 𝔓45 is notorious for its independent text, so one would expect that many readings found in 𝔓45 are suspect. 𝔓45 readings were almost always rejected when supported by A, D, W, *f*1, and *f*13. The only occasion when 𝔓45 readings were accepted into the NA²⁶ text is when the reading was also supported by 𝔓75, B, or ℵ. Likewise, 𝔓46 readings were almost always rejected when 𝔓46 was supported by D and F/G; and 𝔓47 readings were almost always rejected when supported by אֲ versus A and C. It is clear that textual scholars have formed prejudices against certain combinations of manuscripts: $\mathfrak{P}$45, A, D, W, f1, and f13 (versus $\mathfrak{P}$75, אֲ, and B in the Gospels); $\mathfrak{P}$46, D and F/G (versus אֲ, A, and B in the Epistles); and $\mathfrak{P}$47 and אֲ (versus A and C in Revelation). In the NA[26] text, readings supported by these combinations of manuscripts were rarely accepted into the text. However, some of these combined witnesses may represent the original text. And, even if not, they account for no more than one-third of the rejections noted above. That leaves around 650 readings, supported by the earliest manuscripts, relegated to the margin!

There is another disturbing element in NA[26]. In an effort to make NA[26] different from the Westcott and Hort text, the editors rejected nearly 400 readings supported by B that were previously included in the twenty-fifth edition of the Nestle text. In most instances, the B readings have support from other manuscripts (quite often אֲ) and also provide the earliest testimony to a particular variant. But these readings have been relegated to the critical apparatus, while an inferior reading has been left in the text—often enclosed in brackets. Why keep bracketed material in the text when it clearly does not have the support of the earliest manuscripts?

What is noticeable about NA[26] is that the formation of this edition was more influenced by the praxis of eclecticism than the preference for documentation. The result is a text that falls short of recovering the original text of the New Testament because it fails to give full consideration to the testimony of the earliest witnesses.

Modern readers need a text that presents the evidence of the earliest manuscripts. NA[26] does this in part but not fully. Even though many modern scholars would never dare say that anyone could recover the original text of the New Testament, this is exactly what Tregelles, Tischendorf, and Westcott and Hort attempted to do. It is still a worthwhile endeavor and not completely unattainable—if one follows the pattern set by Lachmann, Tregelles, Tischendorf, and Westcott and Hort and then goes on further to make changes based upon the evidence of the earliest manuscripts available today. The Alands realized this but their text (NA[26]) is not completely reflective of this because, in methodology, internal judgments often took precedence over external evidence and there was a conscious movement away from Westcott and Hort. My view is that any early papyrus-supported reading (also having witness from other early manuscripts) is a viable testimony to the original text.

Chapter Ten

An Early Documentary Text and Suggested Revisions for NA^{26} and UBS^3

An Early Documentary Text

The foregoing study has shown that there are several manuscripts that are quite accurate copies of the original text. Most of these were manuscripts produced by early Christian scribes in Egypt or by Christians influenced by Alexandrian scriptoral practices. As the most ancient of textual critics, they were probably in a better position to produce a good copy than modern textual critics. Even though the latter have far more manuscripts at their disposal than the ancients did, the ancients must have had many manuscripts dating from the first and second centuries. The ancients were just as capable in evaluating the quality of manuscripts as modern critics are, and they were much closer to the text—especially with respect to familiarity with the language. Should we not trust that a manuscript produced in Alexandria or by Alexandrian scholarship would be closer to the original than a modern edition?

No one in ancient times read the Greek text that is presented in NA²⁶/UBS³ in its totality—or in any other critical edition of the Greek New Testament, for that matter—because modern critical editions are compilations drawn from multiple manuscripts on a variation-unit by variation-unit basis. This is a legitimate approach to reconstructing the original text, but not the only one.

To avoid the kind of dispersed eclecticism present in NA²⁶/UBS³, which is the product of the local-genealogical method, one could compile a Greek text using whole manuscripts for the basic text for various books or segments of the New Testament. Those manuscripts that are the most reliable would comprise the basic text for a given book or section of the New Testament until they were proven faulty by other documentary evidence or unless they are manifestly faulty in certain places due to scribal error. For example, Matthew 1:1–21 could be an actual reproduction of 𝔓1; Luke 1–6 of 𝔓4; Luke 7–18, 22–24, and John 1–15 of 𝔓75. The lacunae could be filled in with other early papyri, B, or ℵ.

The governing principle for making this kind of text is that the earliest and best manuscripts are generally considered to be representative of the original until proven otherwise. This gives priority of place to external evidence over internal evidence. Unless the internal arguments are overwhelmingly weighted in favor of a reading supported by later manuscripts, the readings supported by the earlier testimony will be accepted into the text. The Greek text produced in such a manner will be more reflective of the earliest testimony of the best manuscripts. Such a documentary presentation would be as follows:

Matthew

1:1–21	𝔓1
2:13–16; 2:22–3:1	𝔓70
3:9–15	𝔓64/67
5:13–16	𝔓86
5:20–22	𝔓64/67
5:22–25	𝔓86
5:25–28	𝔓64/67
11:25–30	𝔓62
(11:26–27	𝔓70)

12:4–5	$\mathfrak{P}$70
19:10–11, 17–18	$\mathfrak{P}$71
23:30–39	$\mathfrak{P}$77
24:3–6, 12–15	$\mathfrak{P}$70
25:12–15, 20–23	$\mathfrak{P}$35
25:43; 26:2–3	($\mathfrak{P}$73?)
26:7–8, 10, 14–15, 22–23, 31–33	$\mathfrak{P}$64/67
gaps filled	B

Mark

2:1–26	$\mathfrak{P}$88
remainder	B

Luke

1:58–59; 1:62–2:1; 2:6–7; 3:8–4:2; 4:29–32, 34–35; 5:3–8; 5:30–6:16	$\mathfrak{P}$4
3:18–4:2; 4:34–5:10; 5:37–18:18; 22:4–24:53	$\mathfrak{P}$75[1]
gaps filled	B

John

1:1–11:45; 11:48–57; 12:3–13:1; 13:8–9; 14:8–30; 15:7–8	$\mathfrak{P}$75
1:1–6:11; 6:35–14:26; 14:29–30; 15:2–26; 16:2–4, 6–7; 16:10–20:20; 20:22–23; 20:25–21:9	$\mathfrak{P}$66[2]

(supplemented by $\mathfrak{P}$5, $\mathfrak{P}$22, $\mathfrak{P}$28, $\mathfrak{P}$39, $\mathfrak{P}$90, 0162)

Acts

2:30–37; 2:46–3:2	$\mathfrak{P}$91
4:31–37	$\mathfrak{P}$8(?)
5:3–21	0189
6:1–6, 8–15	$\mathfrak{P}$8(?)
4:27–17:17 (with many lacunae)	$\mathfrak{P}$45
gaps filled	B

Romans

1:1–7	$\mathfrak{P}$10

1. In the overlap between $\mathfrak{P}$4 and $\mathfrak{P}$75, the latter will generally be given preference.

2. In the overlap between $\mathfrak{P}$66 and $\mathfrak{P}$75, the latter will generally be given preference.

1:24–27; 1:31–2:3; 3:21–4:8; 6:4–5, 16   𝔓40
4:23–5:3; 5:8–13   0220
5:17–6:14; 8:15–15:9; 15:11–16:27   𝔓46
gaps filled   B
(supplemented by 𝔓27 for 8:12–22, 24–27; 8:33–9:3; 9:5–9)

Hebrews   𝔓46
(supplemented by 𝔓13 for 2:14–5:5; 10:8–22; 10:29–11:13;
    11:28–12:7)

1 Corinthians
1:1–16:22   𝔓46
(supplemented by 𝔓15 for 7:18–8:4)

2 Corinthians   𝔓46

Ephesians   𝔓46
(supplemented by 𝔓92 for 1:11–13, 19–21; and by 𝔓49 for
    4:16–29; 4:31–5:13)

Galatians   𝔓46

Philippians   𝔓46
(supplemented by 𝔓16 for 3:10–17; 4:2–8)

Colossians   𝔓46

1 Thessalonians
1:3–2:1; 2:6–13   𝔓65
4:12–13, 16–17; 5:3, 8–10, 12–18,
    25–28   𝔓30
gaps filled   B

2 Thessalonians
1:1–2   𝔓30
1:4–5, 11–12   𝔓92
remainder   B

Titus
1:11–15; 2:3–8   𝔓32
remainder   א

Philemon

13–15, 24–25	𝔓87
remainder	ℵ

James

1:10–12, 15–18	𝔓23
2:19–3:9	𝔓20
remainder	B

1 Peter   𝔓72

(supplemented by 𝔓81 for 2:20–3:1; 3:4–12)

2 Peter   𝔓72

1–3 John   𝔓74 and B

Jude   𝔓74 and B

(supplemented by 𝔓72 for 1–25, and by 𝔓78 for 4–5 and 7–8)

Revelation

1:4–7	𝔓18
5:5–8; 6:5–8	𝔓24
remainder	A

(supplemented by 𝔓47 for 9:10–11:3; 11:5–16:15; 16:17–17:2 and by 𝔓85 for 9:19–10:1; 10:5–9)

Another way to construct a text would be to modify the text of NA²⁶/UBS³ by consistently employing the practice of adopting the testimony of the earliest manuscripts, where two or more of these manuscripts affirm a particular variant reading. For example, the testimony of ℵ and B is to be preferred over all other combinations of later manuscripts. So also the testimony of 𝔓75 and B versus ℵ and later madnuscripts, or 𝔓46 and B versus ℵ and later manuscripts. The testimony would be all the more reliable if there were three early witnesses such as 𝔓75, ℵ, and B—or even two early witnesses plus others of diverse origin, such as 𝔓75, B, and D. Some will argue that the testimony of two early Alexandrian manuscripts is not as potent as that of several manuscripts of various text types. Yet, upon critical examination in most cases, the diverse witnesses often display expansions and editorial tampering, while the Alexandrian manuscripts exhibit the brevity and terseness of the original text.

As was discussed before, the text of NA²⁶/UBS³ falls short of displaying even documentation throughout. The testimony of the early papyri, ℵ, and B was often rejected. NA²⁶/UBS³ would be more reflective of the original text if they followed the testimony of the earliest witnesses. Quite often, these changes would necessitate nothing more than deleting the words, phrases, and verses that are bracketed. These bracketed items, already marked as spurious, should be omitted from the text and relegated to the margin. Their inclusion in the text is almost always based on internal considerations (versus external documentation) or tradition or both.

The following selection of proposed changes is not exhaustive; it is representative of the kind of changes that could be made in NA²⁶/UBS³ to make them more reflective of early documentation. I have selected only those passages where I am fairly certain that the proposed change is defensible primarily on external grounds, but also on internal evidence. At the very least, the internal arguments could easily neutralize one another—therefore forcing a decision based on documentary evidence.

Suggested Revisions for NA²⁶ and UBS³ Based on the Evidence of the Earliest Manuscripts

Matthew 3:7

Omit αὐτοῦ after το βάπτισμα: ℵ* B.

The text would then say that the Pharisees and Sadducees were coming for "the baptism" (i.e., John's baptism).

Matthew 3:16

Omit all bracketed words [αὐτῷ], [τὸ], [τοῦ], [καὶ]: ℵ B.

Thus the text would read, εἶδεν πνεῦμα θεοῦ καταβαῖνον ὡσεὶ περιστερὰν ἐρχόμενον ἐπ' αὐτόν (he saw God's Spirit descending like a dove coming upon him).

Matthew 4:24

Omit [καὶ] (and): B C*.

The text would therefore indicate that the ones suffering

from torments were those who were demon-possessed. These are not two different kinds of people.

Matthew 5:28

Omit αὐτὴν (with her) preceding the phrase ἤδη ἐμοίχευσεν αὐτὴν ἐν τῇ καρδίᾳ αὐτοῦ: 𝔓67 ℵ*.

This then produces the translation, "He has already committed adultery in his heart."

Matthew 9:14

Omit [πολλά] (many): ℵ* B.

This is clearly a scribal addition intended to make a more effective contrast between the fasting of the Pharisees and John's disciples and the lack thereof on the part of Jesus' disciples.

Matthew 13:35

Omit [κόσμου] (of the world): ℵ[1] B.

According to the longer reading, the text says that the prophet spoke "things that were hidden from the foundation of the world," a quotation taken from Psalm 78:2. The Hebrew text says that these things were hidden "from of old"—which in the context of the psalm probably refers to the beginning of the nation of Israel (Carson 1984: 323–24). The Septuagint says that these things were hidden "from the beginning"—which could convey "the beginning of creation." If Matthew was following the Hebrew text here, the shorter reading is more likely original: "These things were hidden from the foundation of Israel." If Matthew was following the Septuagint, the longer reading is more appropriate. The point is this: on the basis of internal evidence, either reading can be argued for. Therefore, we must turn to the external evidence, which clearly favors the omission of κόσμου: ℵ[1], B, *f*1, it[e,k], syr[c,s], Diatessaron[1], Origen (representative witnesses of Alexandrian, Western, and Eastern types of text).

Matthew 16:2b–3

Omit bracketed material: ℵ B cop[sa,bo].

This portion, bracketed in UBS[3] and NA[26], was not written by Matthew, but later inserted by certain scribes who borrowed the concept of the weather as a metaphor for "the signs of the times" from Luke 12:54–56. Had the words been original, there is no reason why the scribes of א and B (also supported by f13, cop^{sa,bo}, arm, and Origen) would have deleted the words on purpose. True, some scholars have argued that the copyists of א and B (both presumed to be of Egypt) omitted these verses because the Egyptian red sky in the morning does not signify the advent of rain. But this is a weak argument for two reasons: (1) we are not sure if א and B were copied in Egypt and (2) even if they were, the copyists would have respected the cultural setting of the Gospel text.

Matthew 21:44

Delete double brackets around this verse: א B C L W Z.

The use of double brackets around certain passages in UBS[3] and NA[26] is supposed to signal to the reader that the enclosed passages are "regarded as later additions to the text" (see UBS[3], p. xlvii). This verse ("the one who falls on this stone will be broken to pieces; and it will crush anyone on whom it falls," NRSV) is said by some scholars to be an interpolation taken from Luke 20:18. However, this argument is not that convincing because one would have expected that the interpolation would have been inserted (quite naturally) after Matthew 21:42, not after 21:43. Besides having strong external testimony, it is very appropriate in this context. Combining the prophecies of Isaiah 8:14–15 and Daniel 2:34–35, 44–45, it depicts Christ as both the Stone over which the Jews stumbled and were broken (see Rom. 9:30–33; 1 Cor. 1:23) and the Stone that will smash all kingdoms in the process of establishing God's kingdom (see Luke 20:43).

Mark 2:5

Change ἀφίενταί (are forgiven), supported by B, to ἀφέωνται (have been forgiven): 𝔓88 א A C D L W 090.

The present tense was probably borrowed from 2:9.

Mark 3:32

Omit [καὶ αἱ ἀδελφαί σου] (and his sisters): א B C L W.

The omission of these words has excellent documentary support. Disagreeing with the decision of the majority of editors of UBS[3] and NA[26], Metzger (1971: 82) writes: "The shorter text preserved in the Alexandrian and Caesarean text-types should be adopted; the longer reading, perhaps of Western origin, crept into the text through mechanical expansion. From a historical point of view, it is extremely unlikely that Jesus' sisters would have joined in publicly seeking to check him in his ministry." It should be pointed out that the omission of "and his sisters" does not indicate that the Bible says that Jesus did not have sisters; he did (see Matt. 13:56; Mark 6:3).

Mark 7:4

Omit [καὶ κλινῶν] (and beds): 𝔓45ᵛⁱᵈ ℵ B L.

These Greek words are included (for the first time in the Nestle text) yet bracketed in UBS³ and NA²⁶ because the committee could not decide if they "were added by copyists who were influenced by the legislation of Lv 15, or whether the words were omitted (a) accidentally because of homoeoteleuton or (b) deliberately because the idea of washing or sprinkling beds seemed to be quite incongruous" (Metzger 1971: 93–94). But whatever the internal arguments, the documentary evidence points to a shorter text.

Mark 14:68

Omit [καὶ ἀλέκτωρ ἐφώνησεν] (and a rooster crowed): ℵ B L W.

Scholars have offered strong arguments both for and against the inclusion of this text on the basis of internal evidence. Those who argue that it was originally written by Mark and then deleted by later scribes say that (1) scribes deleted it to harmonize Mark with Matthew and Luke, who both mention only one cock-crowing and (2) scribes deleted it because it did not make sense to them why Peter would not have repented after hearing the rooster crow. Those who argue that it was not originally written by Mark but added later say that (1) scribes added it because they wanted to emphasize the literal fulfillment of Jesus' prediction in 14:30, and (2) they wanted to account for a first cock-crowing because a second one is mentioned in 14:72. Because the internal arguments are equally persuasive, we have to turn to the external evidence. Clearly, the earliest evidence points to the exclusion of these words.

Mark 16:9–20

Omit verses: ℵ B.

According to the extant documentation, Mark's Gospel (as written by Mark) ends with 16:8. This is attested to by ℵ and B (the two earliest extant manuscripts that preserve this portion of Mark), some early versions (Syriac, Coptic, Armenian, and Georgian), and some early church fathers (Clement, Origen, Eusebius, Jerome, Ammonius, Victor of Antioch, and Euthymius). Each of the various endings that have been appended to Mark 16:1–8 (there are three of them; see UBS[3] for Greek text and the NRSV for English translations) could not have been written by Mark. The most well-known ending, printed as Mark 16:9–20 in UBS[3] and NA[26], is narratively and stylistically incongruous with 16:1–8. Any fair-minded reader can detect its non-Marcan flavor. Major scholarly consensus is that someone other than Mark wrote 16:9–20 perhaps as early as the second century. This writer provided an extended conclusion derived from various sources, including the other Gospels. All the other endings that have been appended are even more obviously not the work of Mark.

The question remains: did Mark originally conclude his Gospel with verse 8 or was an original extended ending lost? Some scholars have recently argued that Mark, given his penchant for terseness, purposely concluded his Gospel at 16:8. But this ending is so abrupt, and doesn't seem to be reflective of Mark's original design. Why conclude with merely an announcement of Jesus' resurrection and a description of the women's fear and bewilderment? In the Gospel of Mark, a pattern is set in which every one of Jesus' predictions is actually fulfilled in narrative form. Thus, since Jesus announced that he would see his disciples in Galilee, the narrative would have depicted an actual appearance of the risen Christ to his disciples in Galilee. Quite likely, the original extended ending had this appearance. But that ending is lost—probably because it was written on the last leaf of a papyrus codex and was torn away from the rest of the manuscript. (As mentioned in chap. 4, the Gospel of Mark may have been the first book of the New Testament to have been published as a codex.)

With respect to the inclusion of the various endings of Mark in the Greek text of UBS[3] and NA[26], it would be better if the text more accurately reflected the evidence of the earliest manuscripts and did, in fact, conclude the Gospel at 16:8. All the endings, then, should be placed in the textual apparatus.

Luke 8:16

Perhaps omit ἵνα οἱ εἰσπορευόμενοι βλέπωσιν τὸ φῶς (that the ones entering may see the light): 𝔓75 B.

This expression is absent in 𝔓75 and B only. One could argue that the scribe of 𝔓75 (followed by the scribe of B) deleted the phrase in order to make Luke 8:16–17 conform to Mark 4:21–22. However, the scribe of 𝔓75 has gained a reputation for being a faithful copyist, and the shorter text of 𝔓75 quite often reflects the original.

Luke 8:43

Omit [ἰατροῖς προσαναλώσασα ὅλον τὸν βίον] (having spent all her living on physicians): 𝔓75 B D syrˢ copˢᵃ.

This expression was probably added from Mark 5:26. Furthermore, it could be argued that Luke, the physician, would not have included a disparaging remark about those in his profession. Internal reasons aside, the documents support the exclusion of this phrase.

Luke 10:21

Perhaps change τῷ πνεύματι τῷ ἁγίῳ (the Holy Spirit), supported by 𝔓75 ℵ B C D L Θ 33, to τῷ πνεύματι (the Spirit [or, the spirit]): 𝔓45ᵛⁱᵈ A W Δ 0115 f13 𝔐 itq goth Clement.

Prior to NA²⁶, the Nestle text displayed the second reading in the text; then the editors of NA²⁶ and UBS³ adopted the first reading. Metzger (1971: 152) provides the rationale for the change: "The strangeness of the expression 'exulted in the Holy Spirit' (for which there is no parallel in the Scriptures) may have led to the omission of τῷ ἁγίῳ from 𝔓45 A W Δ Ψ f13 itq goth Clement al." Indeed, this is a strange expression. The Gospel writers normally did not use the term *Holy Spirit* when speaking of an action that Jesus himself performed ἐν πνεύματι (in spirit). Jesus is said to have "perceived in his spirit" (Mark 2:8), "sighed deeply in his spirit" (Mark 8:12), "grown strong in spirit" (Luke 2:40, some manuscripts), "groaned in the [or his] spirit" (John 11:33), and "been troubled in spirit" (John 13:21). (In grammatical terms, any mention of the word πνεῦμα in the dative case preceded by any verb in the active voice never elsewhere in the Gospels—with respect to Jesus—appears as "the Holy Spirit"—with the exception of the statement about Jesus baptizing "with [or, in] the Holy Spirit.") Whenever the Gospel writers spoke about Jesus' mental or emotional activity related to the S(s)pirit, they viewed it as an activity happening within his spirit. Thus, it would be odd for Luke to say that Jesus "rejoiced in the Holy Spirit."

Must we think that the reading containing this oddity is the original text? Yes, it does have good, early testimony, but so does the shorter reading. I would contend that it is more likely that Luke wrote τῷ πνεύματι and that scribes added ἁγίῳ because (1) scribes had a propensity to add ἁγίῳ to πνεύματι and (2) some scribes may have felt that they wanted to clearly distinguish the "spirit" (πνεῦμα) mentioned in Luke 10:21 from the "spirits" (πνεύματα) mentioned in the previous verse (Luke 10:20, which says, "Do not rejoice in this, that the spirits are subject to you, but rejoice that your names are recorded in heaven"). Given that the second reading could be the original one, Jesus could have been rejoicing in the divine Spirit or in his spirit—the Greek can be taken either way. But it is more likely that Jesus was rejoicing in his spirit.

Luke 11:14

Omit [καὶ αὐτὸ ἦν]: 𝔓45 𝔓75 ℵ A* B L.

Even though Metzger (1971: 158) says that the words καὶ αὐτὸ ἦν κωφόν (and it was mute) appear to be a Semitism in Lukan style, the documentary evidence speaks against their presence in the text.

Luke 11:33

Omit [οὐδὲ ὑπὸ τὸν μόδιον] (or under a bushel): 𝔓45 𝔓75 L 0124.

These Greek words are bracketed in UBS³ and NA²⁶ because they do not appear in the papyri and because they could very well have been borrowed from Matthew 5:15 or Mark 4:21 or both.

Luke 17:24

Omit [ἐν τῇ ἡμέρᾳ αὐτοῦ] (in his day): 𝔓75 B D.

Although the phrase (within the full expression, "the Son of Man in his day") appears in the text of UBS³ and NA²⁶, it is bracketed to signal the editors' doubts about it being originally written by Luke. They had their doubts because the phrase is lacking in 𝔓75, B, and D—which represent early and diverse testimony (Metzger 1971: 167).

Luke 18:11

This verse has a number of variations, translated as follows:

1. the Pharisee standing by himself prayed these things: A W 33ᵛⁱᵈ.
2. the Pharisee stood and prayed these things with [or, about] himself: 𝔓75 ℵ² B L T.
3. the Pharisee stood and prayed these things privately: D.
4. the Pharisee stood and prayed these things: ℵ*.

The editors of UBS³ and NA²⁶ adopted the first reading because in Greek it is the most difficult reading of all the variants, despite the fact that the second reading has the better attestation. I would encourage the adoption of the second reading on the basis of better attestation and clearer expression.

Luke 22:43–44

Omit verses: 𝔓69ᵛⁱᵈ 𝔓75 ℵ¹ B N R T W.

𝔓69ᵛⁱᵈ is not cited in UBS³ in support of the omission of Luke 22:43–44, but it is found in the apparatus of NA²⁶. The editors of 𝔓69 were fairly confident that the only reason to account for the large lacuna in 𝔓69 (from Luke 22:41 to Luke 22:45) would be that the copyist's exemplar did not contain Luke 22:43–44, the passage about Jesus sweating drops of blood while in agony in Gethsemane and then being strengthened by angels. 𝔓69ᵛⁱᵈ adds another early witness to the omission of this text; indeed, it is not found in the manuscripts mentioned above or in Marcion, Clement, or Origen. The earliest witness to the inclusion of this passage is 0170 (which actually shows only the last few words of Luke 22:44)—a D-type text dated around 300, followed by ℵ* (dated 350–375). Other early testimony comes from some early church fathers (Justin, Irenaeus, Hippolytus, Dionysius, and Eusebius) who acknowledged this portion as part of Luke's Gospel.

The debate about the genuineness of this passage focused on whether Jesus needed to be strengthened by angels during his trial in the garden of Gethsemane. Some said that the passage was excised because certain Christians who thought that "the account of Jesus overwhelmed with human weakness was incompatible with his sharing the divine omnipotence of the Father" (Metzger 1971: 177). But it is more likely that the passage was an early (second-century) interpolation, added from an oral tradition concerning the life of Jesus (Westcott and Hort 1882: appendix pp. 64–67).

Luke 23:34

Omit bracketed material: $\mathfrak{P}$75 $\aleph$[1vid] B D* W 0124.

The omission of this famous saying ("And Jesus said, 'Father, forgive them, for they do not know what they are doing'")— evident in early and diverse manuscripts (the earliest being $\mathfrak{P}$75)—cannot be explained as a scribal blunder or as a purposeful scribal excision. Good reasons cannot be posited for either. Rather, it appears that this text was not a part of Luke's original writing, but was added later (as early as the second century— for it is attested to by Hegesippus, Marcion, the Diatessaron, and Justin) from an oral tradition. (This is the position expressed by Westcott and Hort 1882: appendix pp. 67–69; and Metzger 1971: 180.) The words appear in the text of UBS[3] and NA[26] but are bracketed to signal the editors' hesitancy to include them as part of Luke's original writing and thereby demonstrate their respect for the testimony of $\mathfrak{P}$75 with $\aleph$[1vid], B, D*, and W.

John 1:19

Omit [πρὸς αὐτὸν] (to him): $\mathfrak{P}$66 $\mathfrak{P}$75.

The documentary evidence shows clearly that this phrase is a scribal addition, inserted by scribes to provide an indirect object after the verb ἀπέστειλαν (sent). The transposition of this phrase also makes the reading suspect as a scribal addition. The editors of NA[26] retained it in the text (in brackets) in preference to the testimony of B.

John 1:34

Perhaps change ὁ υἱὸς τοῦ θεοῦ (the Son of God), supported by $\mathfrak{P}$66 $\mathfrak{P}$75 A B C W 083, to ὁ ἐκλεκτός τοῦ θεοῦ (the Chosen One of God): $\mathfrak{P}$5[vid] $\aleph$*.

Several scholars have argued that it is more likely that the reading "the Chosen One of God" was changed to "the Son of God" than vice versa. For example, Gordon Fee (1979: 431–32) thinks an orthodox scribe of the second century might have sensed "the possibility that the designation 'Chosen One' might be used to support adoptionism" and so altered the text "for orthodox reasons" (see also Williams 1974). Furthermore, the title *Chosen One* adds one more messianic title to the chain of witnesses in John 1, while *Son* is repetitive (see 1:14, 49). Christ as the Word is called God (1:1, 18 [in the earliest manuscripts]; see Isa. 9:6); and Jesus is called the Christ or Messiah (1:17, 41; see Ps. 2:2; Dan. 9:25), the Son of God (1:34 [in some manuscripts], 49; see 2 Sam. 7:12–14; Ps. 2:7), the Lamb of God (1:29, 36; see Isa. 53), the one predicted by Moses (1:45; see Deut. 18:16–18), the King of Israel (1:49; see Ps. 2:6; Zeph. 3:15), and the Son of Man (1:51; see Dan. 7:13). If the title the *Chosen One of God* also came from the pen of John, this is yet another messianic witness, referring to Isaiah 42:1. (It should be noted that all the other Gospel accounts concerning Jesus' baptism by John contain a record of God's utterance from heaven: "This is my beloved Son, in whom I am well pleased"—an utterance echoing Isa. 42:1: "Here is my servant, whom I uphold, my chosen one in whom I delight.")

John 4:1

Change Ἰησοῦς, supported by ℵ D, to κύριος: 𝔓66 𝔓75 A B C L W (𝔓66 may have originally read Ἰησοῦς).

The first reading ("Jesus") is the more difficult one, and therefore the one adopted by UBS³ and NA²⁶ (a change from previous editions of the Nestle text). But, in this case the superior testimony of 𝔓66, 𝔓75, A, B, C, L, and W should be given priority. Besides, it could be argued that scribes changed κύριος to Ἰησοῦς because the name Ἰησοῦς immediately follows twice—without consciously knowing they had created a more difficult reading.

John 4:35–36

Punctuate as θερισμόν ἤδη. ὁ θερίζων . . . : 𝔓75.

The punctuation in UBS³ and NA²⁶ has a period between θερισμόν and ἤδη (already). According to the punctuation in 𝔓75, these verses should read as, "Look on the fields that they are *already* white for harvest. He who reaps is receiving wages, and is gathering fruit to eternal life."

John 5:44

Change τοῦ μόνου θεοῦ (the only God), supported by ℵ A D, to τοῦ μόνου (the unique one): 𝔓66 𝔓75 B.

According to E. A. Abbott, the expression found in 𝔓66 and 𝔓75 could be written as a title, τοῦ μόνου—"the only one" or "the unique one." Abbott (1906:11) writes: "When speaking about 'glory' and its source, the evangelist used ὁ μόνος—with allusion to the connexion of the word with 'glory' both in Hebrew and Greek—to mean briefly 'He that is *alone* glorious,' i.e. 'He from whom *alone* glory comes.'"

John 7:53–8:11

Omit verses: 𝔓66 𝔓75 A^vid ℵ B C^vid T W.

The pericope about the adulterous woman is not included in any of the earliest manuscripts. Its first appearance in a Greek manuscript is in D (fifth/sixth century), but it is not contained in other Greek manuscripts until the ninth century. The story is known in three different versions: one known to Papias, one in the Gospel according to the Hebrews, and the popular version found in later manuscripts, where it appears in different places: after John 7:52, after Luke 21:38, or at the end of John; and when it does appear it is often marked off by asterisks or obeli to signal its probable spuriousness. The story is part of an oral tradition that was included in the Syriac Peshitta, circulated in the Western church, eventually finding its way into the Latin Vulgate, and from there into later Greek manuscripts, the likes of which were used in formulating the Textus Receptus.

The external evidence against the Johannine authorship of the pericope about the adulteress is overwhelming. The internal evidence against Johannine authorship is also impressive. First of all, many scholars have pointed out that the vocabulary used in this pericope does not accord with the rest of John. Second, the insertion of the pericope at this point in John (after John 7:52 and before John 8:12) greatly disrupts the narrative flow. Westcott and Hort indicated that the setting of John 7 and 8 is at Jerusalem during the Feast of Tabernacles. During this feast, the Jews would customarily pour water over a rock (in commemoration of the water supply coming from the smitten rock in the wilderness) and light lamps (in commemoration of the pillar of light that accompanied the Israelites in their wilderness journey). With reference to these two ritualistic enactments, Jesus presented himself as the true source of living water (John 7:37–39) and as the true light to be followed (John 8:12).

In addition to these arguments, it can also be said that the pericope concerning the adulteress interrupts the connection between John 7:40–52 and 8:12. John 8:12 contains a response—even though indirect—to John 7:52. In John 8:12 Jesus began speaking to the Pharisees who had boldly told Nicodemus that the Scriptures make no mention of even a prophet (much less the Christ) being raised up in Galilee. With respect to this assertion, Jesus made a declaration in which he implied that the Scriptures did speak of the Christ coming from Galilee. He said, "I am the light of the world. Whoever follows me will never walk in darkness, but will have the light of life." This statement was probably drawn from Isaiah 9:1–2, which contains images parallel to those in John 8:12. Both speak about the light, walking in darkness, and the shadow of death versus the light of life. This parallel thereby provides a reproof to the Pharisees' declaration in John 7:52 (see Westcott and Hort 1882: appendix pp. 82–88; Metzger 1971: 219–22; Comfort 1989).

John 9:4

Change πέμψαντός με (sent me), supported by ℵ¹ A B C D, to πέμψαντος ἡμᾶς (sent us): 𝔓66 𝔓75 ℵ* L W.

John 9:4 provides an excellent example of how uneven the documentary presentation is in UBS³ and NA²⁶. In the first part of this verse, the testimony of 𝔓66, 𝔓75, ℵ, B, L, and W is accepted for the reading ἡμᾶς δεῖ ἐργάζεσθαι (it is necessary for us to work)—versus ἐμὲ δεῖ ἐργάζεσθαι (it is necessary for me to work). But in the next part of the verse, the testimony of 𝔓66, 𝔓75, ℵ*, L, and W is rejected supporting the reading πέμψαντος ἡμᾶς (sent us). Metzger (1971: 227) claims that πέμψαντος ἡμᾶς is a non-Johannine expression that was introduced as correlative to ἡμᾶς δεῖ ἐργάζεσθαι at the beginning of the verse. But it is the very unusualness of the expression that caused later scribes to change ἡμᾶς to με here—and in the last part of the verse. The entire verse, according to the earliest manuscript evidence, says, "It is necessary for us to work the works of him who sent us while it is day." Once the text is established—no matter how unusual—we can then seek to explicate it. In the context, it seems that Jesus was including his disciples as coworkers, who (together with him) were sent by God to carry out God's work. (Compare the use of the plural in 3:11.)

John 9:38–39a

Omit verses: 𝔓75 ℵ* W.

This portion is not included in 𝔓75, ℵ*, W, Codex Veronensis (Old Latin "b"), and the Diatessaron. It could be argued that the omission may be the result of a transcriptional error (haplography)—the eye of some scribes went from "Jesus said to him" in 9:37 to "and Jesus said" in 9:39 and continued copying from there. However, it is somewhat more likely that 9:38–39a is an early liturgical addition to the text. Brown (1966: 375) suggests that the words may be "an addition stemming from the association of John ix with the baptismal liturgy and catechesis." This is also the view of Porter (1967).

John 10:29

Change ὁ πατήρ μου ὃ δέδωκέν μοι πάντων μεῖζόν ἐστιν (that which my Father has given me is greater than all), supported by B, to ὁ πατήρ μου ὃς δέδωκέν μοι πάντων μείζων ἐστίν (my Father, who has given them to me, is greater than all): 𝔓66ᶜ 𝔓75ᵛⁱᵈ.

𝔓75 clearly read ὅς but deterioration has marred the word μεῖζον/μείζων. Perhaps this accounts for the fact that neither UBS³ nor NA²⁶ cite 𝔓75 in the apparatus along with 𝔓66. When I pointed this out to Dr. Aland, I was told that 𝔓75 will be added to the apparatus of NA²⁶ in a future printing, even though this will necessitate restructuring the entire note to accommodate the evidence of 𝔓75. In all likelihood, therefore, 𝔓75 supports the reading that can be rendered, "My Father, who has given them to me, is greater than all" (see Comfort 1990b). This reading is more natural than the one supported by B, which reads, "That which my Father has given me is greater than all"—even though it is the more difficult reading and can be explained to indicate that the church (given to the Son by the Father) is greater than its enemies.

John 13:2

Change γινομένου, supported by ℵ* B, to γενομένου: 𝔓66 ℵ² A D.

The difference between these two variants involves a single letter in the Greek text: "supper happening" versus "supper having happened" (or, taken as an ingressive aorist, "supper having been served"). If the second reading cannot be understood as an ingressive aorist, the statement contradicts the context, which clearly indicates that the supper was in progress.

John 13:32

Omit [εἰ ὁ θεὸς ἐδοξάσθη ἐν αὐτῷ] (if God was glorified in him): 𝔓66 ℵ* B C* D W.

None of the earliest manuscripts contain this first part of John 13:32. Nevertheless, many scholars think that it is an intrinsic part of John's original writing and that it was omitted from many manuscripts because of homoeoteleuton—deliberate deletion of perceived redundancy (see John 13:31). On the other hand, it could be argued that the words were added to create a protasis. Again, the decision should be made on the basis of external evidence, which points to the omission of this phrase.

John 19:35

Change πιστεύσητε, supported by ℵ² A Dˢ W, to πιστεύητε: 𝔓66ᵛⁱᵈ (not cited in NA²⁶) ℵ* B.

The present subjunctive πιστεύητε is more characteristically Johannine; it suggests a continual believing—as opposed to the aorist, which suggests initial faith. (See comments on John 20:31.)

John 20:31

Change πιστεύσητε, supported by ℵ² A C D W, to πιστεύητε: 𝔓66ᵛⁱᵈ ℵ* B.

In both 19:35 and 20:31, 𝔓66ᵛⁱᵈ (with ℵ* and B) reads the present subjunctive πιστεύητε (may continue to believe). Other manuscripts (ℵ², A, D, L, and W) read the aorist πιστεύσητε. The editors of UBS³ and NA²⁶ followed this reading, but signaled their doubt about the aorist verb by bracketing the sigma: πιστεύ[σ]ητε. Given John's tendency to use the present tense verb when speaking about a continual believing, a believing that extends beyond the initial act of faith, it seems more likely that John here wrote the present subjunctive, not the aorist. In these verses John was certifying the trustworthiness of his testimony so that the readers (who were probably already believers) would continue to believe the veracity of the gospel.

Acts 3:6

Omit [ἔγειρε καὶ] (arise and): ℵ B D cop[sa].

The insertion of these words in the statement made by Peter to the lame man ("in the name of Jesus Christ, the Nazarene, [arise and] walk") was introduced by scribes who were influenced by the formula "arise and walk" so common in the Gospels (see Matt. 9:5; Mark 2:9; Luke 5:23; John 5:8).

Acts 13:33

There are three variant readings in this verse pertaining to the identification of the psalm quoted by Paul: (1) second psalm: 𝔓74 ℵ A B C E 33; (2) first psalm: D and some Old Latin manuscripts; (3) psalms: 𝔓45.

The first and second psalms (as we know them in our English Bibles) were often put together as one psalm in the Hebrew text. Metzger (1971: 412–14) provides a lengthy discussion concerning the textual problem here. Good reasons are advanced for each of the readings, but in the final analysis the editors of UBS[3] and NA[26] (as well as almost all the translators) prefer the testimony of the four great uncials over against D or 𝔓45. However, I would prefer the testimony of 𝔓45 against all the other manuscripts because it is the oldest extant manuscript containing Acts and because it best explains the other readings.

Romans 8:28

Change πάντα συνεργεῖ εἰς ἀγαθόν (everything works together for good [or, he works everything together for good]), supported by ℵ C D 33 1739, to πάντα συνεργεῖ ὁ θεός εἰς ἀγαθόν (God works everything together for good): 𝔓46 A B.

It has been argued that the scribes of 𝔓46, A, and B added "God" to the existing text in order to clarify an ambiguous text, reflected in the first reading above, where the subject could be "everything" or "he." In the context of Romans 8, it would seem that the subject is "God" or "the Spirit" (both are mentioned in Rom. 8:27). God or the Spirit is the one who works all things together for good. Of the two, God is the more natural subject—and one that Paul very likely wrote.

1 Corinthians 7:40

𝔓15 and 33 contain the reading "the Spirit of Christ," whereas all the other manuscripts have the reading "the Spirit of God."

Given the good textual character of 𝔓15 (and 33), should not its reading be given some consideration? The title *Spirit of Christ* is far less common than *Spirit of God*; the former appears only in Romans 8:9 and 1 Peter 1:11, the latter in many New Testament verses. It would be much more likely that scribes changed "the Spirit of Christ" to "the Spirit of God" than vice versa. In this chapter Paul has made the point of separating his advice from the Lord's directives (see 7:10, 25). Nonetheless, he claims that his advice concerning virgins and the unmarried is to be heeded because he has the Spirit of God/Christ. Having made the Lord (i.e., the Lord Jesus Christ) the source of reference throughout this chapter, Paul would have found it natural to conclude with an affirmation of his possession of "the Spirit of Christ" rather than "the Spirit of God." All these arguments, it must be admitted, cannot completely outweigh the fact that all the other manuscripts read "the Spirit of God." Nevertheless, some modern versions would do well to list this reading in the margin.

1 Corinthians 10:2

Change ἐβαπτίσθησαν (were baptized), supported by ℵ A C D 33, to ἐβαπτίσαντο (received baptism): 𝔓46ᶜ B 1739.

The first reading is a passive voice verb; the second, a middle voice. The first reading was adopted by the majority of UBS³ and NA²⁶ editors, with Bruce Metzger and Allen Wikgren voicing the minority view. According to Metzger and Wikgren, the reading in 𝔓46ᶜ, B, and 1739 is more likely Pauline because the Jews baptized themselves (conveyed by the middle voice), whereas Christians were baptized by others (conveyed by the passive voice)—and Christian scribes would be more likely to change the middle voice to the passive than vice versa (see Metzger 1971: 559).

1 Corinthians 15:49

Change φορέσομεν καὶ τὴν εἰκόνα τοῦ ἐπουρανίου (we shall also bear the image of the heavenly), supported by B I, to φορέσωμεν καὶ τὴν εἰκόνα τοῦ ἐπουρανίου (let us also bear the image of the heavenly): 𝔓46 ℵ A C D 33 1739.

Metzger (1971: 569) argues that the first reading best suits the context—which is didactic, not hortatory. But Fee counters this textual decision, arguing that it was far more likely that scribes changed the hortatory ("let us bear") to the future ("we shall bear"). Therefore, Fee (1987: 795) argues that the second reading "must be the original, and if original it must be intentional on Paul's part as a way of calling them [the Corinthians] to prepare now for the future that is to be."

2 Corinthians 1:10

Change τηλικούτου θανάτου (so great a death), supported by ℵ A B C D 33 1739* Clement, to τηλικούτου θανάτων (so great deaths): 𝔓46 1739ᶜ Origen.

Zuntz (1953: 104) argues for the reading in 𝔓46, which is plural, translating the phrase "out of such tremendous, mortal dangers." Robert G. Bratcher (1983: 11), who translated the New Testament portion of Today's English Version, also supports the plural, rendering the phrase, "such terrible dangers of death."

2 Corinthians 1:12

Change ἁπλότητι (simplicity [or, sincerity]), supported by ℵ² D, to ἁγιότητι (holiness): 𝔓46 ℵ* A B C 33 1739.

In Greek, one word could have easily been confused for the other because the two words differ in only two letters (πλ/γι). The first reading, adopted for the text of NA26 (a change from previous editions of the Nestle text) and UBS³, was selected because the context seems to call for a word that describes Paul's forthrightness in handling the contribution from the Gentile churches to the saints in Jerusalem (see 1:11; see Martin 1986: 18). However, the word ἁγιότητι also suits the context—for Paul was speaking of having a sanctified behavior "in this world" (see Thrall 1976). Because ἁγιότητι is a word Paul never uses elsewhere, scribes changed it to ἁπλότητι (used a number of times in 2 Cor.—8:2; 9:11, 13; 11:3). Again, the internal evidence is balanced, but not so the external: ἁπλότητι is a Western and Byzantine reading (given a "D" rating in UBS³), whereas ἁγιότητι has the support of all the earliest Alexandrian witnesses.

Galatians 1:3

Change θεοῦ πατρὸς ἡμῶν καὶ κυρίου Ἰησοῦ Χριστοῦ (God our Father and Lord Jesus Christ), supported by א A 33, to θεοῦ πατρὸς καὶ κυρίου ἡμῶν Ἰησοῦ Χριστοῦ (God the Father and our Lord Jesus Christ): 𝔓46 𝔓51ᵛⁱᵈ B D 1739.

The editors of UBS³ and NA²⁶ adopted the first reading because it accords with Paul's usual style (see Rom. 1:7; 1 Cor. 1:3; 2 Cor. 1:2; Eph. 1:2; Phil. 1:2). But the papyri and B evidence another reading, which could have very well been changed by scribes to accord with Paul's usual formula.

Galatians 1:15

Change εὐδόκησεν ὁ θεός (God was pleased), supported by א A D 33 1739, to εὐδόκησεν (he was pleased): 𝔓46 B.

The title ὁ θεός (God) is bracketed in UBS³ and NA²⁶ to signal the editors' doubts about its inclusion in the text (it was not present in the previous editions of the Nestle text). They were influenced by the testimony of 𝔓46 and B, whose text does not specify the subject as "God."

Ephesians 1:1

Omit [ἐν Ἐφέσῳ] (in Ephesus): 𝔓46 א* B* 1739.

In the Greek texts of UBS³ and NA²⁶, these words have been bracketed to show that the editors had good reason to doubt that they were written by Paul. Indeed, the three earliest manuscripts (𝔓46, א, and B) do not have these words; the phrase may then be translated, "To the saints who are faithful in Christ Jesus." If this is the way it originally read, Paul could have very well intended this epistle to be a general encyclical sent to the churches in Asia, of which Ephesus was one of the leading churches. No doubt, the epistle would have gone to Ephesus (perhaps first) and then on to other churches. Each time the epistle went to another church, the name of the locality would be supplied after the expression "to the saints [in ———]." Zuntz indicates that this procedure also occurred with some multiple copies of royal letters during the Hellenistic period; the master copy would have a blank for the addressee that would be filled in for each copy. Thus, Zuntz (1953: 228 n. 1) considers the blank space in the address to the Ephesians as going back to the original. The very content of this epistle affirms its general nature, for it lacks the usual references to local situations and persons (as found in Paul's other epistles).

But whatever the arguments concerning the intrinsic nature of this textual variant, the documentary evidence points to the absence of the phrase *in Ephesus*. The three earliest manuscripts do not have the phrase, and later scribes added the phrase to ℵ and B. Given this evidence, the words should not have been included in UBS³ or NA²⁶ (even bracketed).

Ephesians 4:28

Change ἐργαζόμενος ταῖς [ἰδίας] χερσὶν (working with his own hands), supported by ℵ* A D, to ἐργαζόμενος ταῖς χερσὶν (working with his hands): 𝔓46 𝔓49ᵛⁱᵈ ℵ² B.

The Greek word ἰδίας (own) has been bracketed in UBS³ and NA²⁶ to show the editors' doubts about its right to be in the text. Surely, the manuscript evidence is against it, but the editors included it on the grounds that it represents Koine usage (Metzger 1971: 605–6).

Philippians 3:3

There are three variants in this verse, which translate as follows: (1) who worship by [or, in] the Spirit of God: ℵ* A B C D² 33 1739; (2) who worship God in spirit: ℵ² D*; (3) who worship in spirit: 𝔓46.

According to Greek grammar, the first reading (οἱ πνεύματι θεοῦ λατρεύοντες) can be rendered "the ones worshiping by the Spirit of God" or "the ones worshiping the Spirit of God." In Greek, the verb λατρεύω (worship) is normally followed by the dative (in this verse, πνεύματι, Spirit); hence, the Spirit becomes the recipient of the worship. Since the grammar allows a rendering that might be offensive to those who do not think the Spirit should be worshiped, some scribes added another object in the dative case, θεῷ (God)—hence, the second reading noted above. But Lightfoot demonstrates that the verb λατρεύω had acquired a technical sense referring to the worship of God and therefore one does not have to understand the phrase *the Spirit of God* as the object of the worship (see Lightfoot 1891: 145; and Kent 1978: 144). Thus, many commentators and translators understand the phrase to function as a dative. The earliest manuscript, 𝔓46, does not have any object after the participle and is very likely the original text. The bare expression οἱ πνεύματι λατρεύοντες of necessity means "to worship God" (Hawthorne 1983: 122).

Colossians 3:6

Omit [ἐπὶ τοὺς υἱοὺς τῆς ἀπειθείας] (upon the sons of disobedience): 𝔓46 B.

This phrase was included in UBS³ and NA²⁶ (a change from previous editions of the Nestle text) but set within brackets to show the editors' doubts about its authenticity. It is not present in 𝔓46 and B, having every appearance of being assimilated from Ephesians 5:6.

1 Thessalonians 5:9

𝔓30, B, and a few early versions read "salvation through our Lord Jesus"—versus all the other manuscripts, which read "salvation through our Lord Jesus Christ."

The NA²⁶ and UBS³ Greek texts adhere to the second reading—as do all the versions. But given the fact that scribes tended to add names to divine titles and that the two earliest manuscripts do not contain the word *Christ*, is it not possible that 𝔓30 and B contain the original reading?

Hebrews 3:2

Change ἐν [ὅλῳ] τῷ οἴκῳ αὐτοῦ (in all his house), supported by ℵ A C D, to ἐν τῷ οἴκῳ αὐτοῦ (in his house): 𝔓13 𝔓46 B.

The first reading exactly follows Numbers 12:7 in the Septuagint and perfectly accords with Hebrews 3:5. These two facts, however, can be used to defend the second reading—for one can argue that the scribes of ℵ, A, C, and D conformed the text to one or the other of these passages.

Hebrews 12:3

Change ὑπὸ τῶν ἁμαρτωλῶν εἰς ἑαυτὸν ἀντιλογίαν (opposition by sinners against sinners), supported by A Dᶜ 1739ᶜ, to ὑπὸ τῶν ἁμαρτωλῶν εἰς ἑαυτοὺς ἀντιλογίαν (opposition by sinners against them[selves]): 𝔓13 𝔓46 ℵ D* 048 33 1739.

The second reading, though not included in the text of NA[26] nor adopted by any of the modern versions, is definitely the earlier and harder reading—and therefore is to be preferred. The passage would then mean that Jesus received "opposition from sinners against themselves"—that is, sinners doing hurt to themselves by opposing Jesus (see Prov. 8:36; see Morris 1981: 135).

1 Peter 2:21

Perhaps change ἔπαθεν (suffered), supported by 𝔓72 A B C 33 1739, to ἀπέθανεν (died): 𝔓81 ℵ.

As in 1 Peter 3:18 (see comments below), there is a textual variation in this verse as to whether Christ "suffered" for sins or "died" for sins. In 1 Peter 2:21, 𝔓81 (not cited in UBS[3]) adds another early witness for the reading "died"—against the evidence of the early papyrus 𝔓72. This creates the situation with 𝔓72 and B versus 𝔓81 and ℵ in a virtual standoff.

1 Peter 3:18

Change ἔπαθεν (suffered), supported by B P, to ἀπέθανεν (died): 𝔓72 ℵ A C^vid 33 1739.

Like 1 Peter 2:21, in which the context seems to favor the reading "suffered" instead of "died" (see comments above), it would seem natural for Peter (again speaking about suffering— see 3:14–18) to say that Christ "suffered for sins" rather than "died for sins." But the evidence of 𝔓72 with ℵ, A, and C offsets the testimony of B. Furthermore, the second reading in this context is the more difficult reading and therefore the one more likely to have been changed.

2 Peter 1:3

Change καλέσαντος ἡμᾶς ἰδίᾳ δόξῃ καὶ ἀρετῇ (called us by [or, to] his own glory and virtue), supported by ℵ A C 33 1739, to καλέσαντος ἡμᾶς διὰ δόξης καὶ ἀρετῆς (called us through his glory and virtue): 𝔓72 B.

The difference in the two readings is very slight in the Greek; in fact, there is only a one-letter difference ἰδίᾳ (to his own) versus διὰ (through), plus the final sigmas on the two nouns to indicate the genitive case. Both readings have good support and are suitable to the context—for God did call the believers to participate in his own glory and virtue, or he did so by means of expressing his glory and virtue through his Son.

Jude 5

There are four variant readings in this verse, which translate as follows: (1) the Lord delivered his people out of Egypt: ℵ C* L; (2) Jesus delivered his people out of Egypt: A B 33 1739; (3) God, the Messiah, delivered his people out of Egypt: 𝔓72; (4) God delivered his people out of Egypt: C².

Among all the readings cited above, the second reading is the most remarkable, for it says that "*Jesus* delivered his people out of Egypt." This reading is found in A, B, 33, 1739, some early Coptic manuscripts, Origen, and Bede. 𝔓72 is possibly an indirect witness to this reading because it shows that the scribe had before him (in his exemplar) a messianic title—"Messiah" or "Christ." At any rate, it is easier to argue (from a textual perspective) that the reading with "Jesus" is the one from which all the others deviated than to argue that the reading with "Lord" (or "God") was changed to "Jesus." Scribes were not known for fabricating difficult readings.

Conceivably Jude wrote Ἰησοῦς in verse 5 as a reference to Joshua (as in Heb. 4:8)—the Greek names for Jesus and Joshua are identical—but this is very unlikely. Joshua led the Israelites into the good land but not out of Egypt, and he certainly did not destroy those who did not believe (v. 5b). Given the fact that Jude was writing from a New Testament perspective, a perspective that viewed Jesus as being Yahweh the Savior, it is not difficult to imagine that Jude would say that Jesus delivered the Israelites out of Egypt (see 1 Cor. 10:4, 9). Thus, several scholars are convinced that Jude wrote "Jesus" (see Alford 1871: 532; Nestle 1901: 328–29; Bruce 1968: 35–36; and Wikgren 1967).

Though the reading with "Jesus" seems to be the one Jude wrote, not one translation has adopted this reading for the text. Rather, it has been usually relegated to the margin. The first edition of the UBS *Greek New Testament* contained the reading "Jesus" in the text. But this changed in the third edition, when a slim majority of the editors voted to put the reading with "Lord" in the text and the one with "Jesus" in the margin. (Metzger and Wikgren voted against this decision and stated their reasons for doing so in Metzger 1971: 724.)

Revelation 14:3

Change ᾄδουσιν [ὡς] ᾠδὴν καινὴν (they sing, as it were, a new song), supported by A C, to ᾄδουσιν ᾠδὴν καινὴν (they sing a new song): 𝔓47 ℵ.

The Greek word for "as it were" [ὡς] has been bracketed in UBS³ and NA²⁶ (it was not included in previous editions of the Nestle text); no doubt the word was included because of its presence in A and C, but bracketed because of its absence in 𝔓47 and ℵ.

Revelation 15:3

Change ὁ βασιλεὺς τῶν ἐθνῶν (King of the nations), supported by ℵ¹ A P, to ὁ βασιλεὺς τῶν αἰώνων (King of the ages): 𝔓47 ℵ*,² C.

Those who prefer the first reading can argue that the second reading was adopted from 1 Timothy 1:17, whereas the first reading is a unique expression in the New Testament. But it can also be argued that the words *the nations* in the next verse caused the scribes to change "ages" to "nations" (Tasker 1964: 444). Thus, arguments pertaining to internal considerations are offsetting. With respect to the documentary evidence, the testimony of 𝔓47 with ℵ* and C demonstrates weightier external support than does ℵ¹ and A.[3]

3. Some portions of this chapter were adopted from my 1990 book.

Textual Evidence for the Earliest Edition of John's Gospel: Examining 𝔓5 and 𝔓75

As was noted above, it is thought that several books of the New Testament were published in various editions. While debate continues on books like Acts and Paul's epistles, most New Testament scholars are convinced that the Gospel of John was produced in (at least) two editions: one with twenty chapters and a second with an appended epilogue, the twenty-first chapter. However, all the scholars who advocate the two editions have done so without any textual evidence. In fact, scholars candidly confess that there is no textual evidence to substantiate two editions. For example, D. A. Carson in a recent commentary on the Gospel of John (1991: 667–68) says, "There is no textual evidence that the book was ever published without John 21. Certainly if the first twenty chapters of the book had been published for a few years before ch. 21 was added, one would expect significant textual evidence of such independent circulation." Thus, since no one (as of yet) has shown there to be any textual evidence for two or more editions, all suppositions have been based on internal literary evidence—as opposed to external textual evidence (see Parker

1956). But there is reason to believe that $\mathfrak{P}5$ (Oxyrhynchus Papyri 208 and 1781) and $\mathfrak{P}75$ (Bodmer Papyrus XIV–XV) provide evidence of a gospel with only twenty chapters.

$\mathfrak{P}5$

The Oxyrhynchus papyrus designated $\mathfrak{P}5$ has two sections—the first published as Oxyrhynchus Papyrus 208, the second as 1781. The fragment designated 208 contains in one leaf (folded in half) John 1:23–31 on a recto and 1:33–41 on a verso; with 20:11–17 on a verso and 20:19–20, 22–25 on a recto. The fragment designated 1781 contains 16:14–22a on a recto and 16:22b–30 on a verso. The editors, Grenfell and Hunt, assume (1898–: 2.1) that the gospel in this manuscript must have contained twenty-one chapters:

> If, then, the original book contained the whole of the Gospel, which is certainly the most natural supposition, our sheet was very nearly the outermost of a large quire, and within it were a number of other sheets sufficient to hold the eighteen intervening chapters. Written upon the same scale as the surviving fragments, these eighteen chapters would fill twenty-two sheets. The whole book would thus consist of a single quire of twenty-five sheets, the first leaf being probably left blank, or giving only the title. Such an arrangement certainly seems rather awkward, particularly as the margin between the two columns of writing in the flattened sheet is only about 2 cm. wide.

The reconstruction of the format of $\mathfrak{P}5$ as given by Grenfell and Hunt is problematic because they were trying to account for a twenty-one-chapter gospel. First of all, it is very unlikely that a scribe would leave an entire leaf blank (on both sides) or use it just for the title. Furthermore, it is not likely that the scribe could fit a twenty-one-chapter gospel within the page allotment of this manuscript. According to my calculations, the scribe fit about 700 characters (maximum) per page (27 lines per page and 26 characters per line). I arrived at this number by counting the number of characters for (1) the partial page that contains 1:23–31+ (approximately 690 characters, given the addition of the lacunae), (2) the full page that contains 16:14–22a (711 characters), and (3) the full page that contains 16:22b–30 (685 characters, with a small corrigenda at the bottom). $\mathfrak{P}5$ ends with John 20:25a. The Greek text in UBS[3] (taking into account *nomina sacra*) has about 3,190 characters from John 20:25a to the end of 21:25. If the manuscript contained twenty-one chapters, the words could not fit in the format suggested by Grenfell and Hunt because the most a scribe could fit would be about 180 characters on the same page as 20:19–20, 22–25, and then another 2,800 on the next four pages—totalling 2,980. This is 210 characters short—and the number is very likely be more. It is possible that the scribe could have seen that he was going to run out of room; so he may have squeezed in the last two-and-a-half verses. But that would mean he would have had to fit about eight more lines on the page.[1]

In defense of a twenty-one-chapter format, it should be said that two more sheets could have been added at the end of the scribe's task when he saw that he did not have enough room to fit the full twenty-one chapters. This is adequately described by Sanders (1938: 74–75):

> Another possible arrangement is suggested by P. Oxy. 208, a double papyrus leaf containing John 1,23–31 and 33–41 on the first leaf and 20,11–17 and 19–25 on the second. As was shown by the editors, this implies a single quire of at least 25 sheets or 50 leaves of which the whole first leaf was blank or contained only the title on the inside page, i.e., the recto. This may have been the original arrangement of the papyrus codex before a binding was considered a necessity, or this may be another example of a papyrus codex, in which the original plan was exceeded by one or more sheets in order to include all of the text of the book. As in the single quire codex form the first leaf of each double sheet had to be written before any of the leaves of the second half, any miscalculation which forced the adding of one or more leaves at the end must cause that number of blank leaves to be added at the beginning. As I consider John Chap. 21 genuine, so I must hold that this manuscript contained it. In that case the manuscript consisted of twenty-six double sheets and two whole leaves were blank at the beginning.

Sanders's calculation coincides with mine: in order to fit all of chapter 21 at the end of the codex, the scribe would have had to add *two* more sheets (not *one* as conjectured by Grenfell and Hunt)—thereby making two entire blank leaves (both sides) at

---

1. 𝔓5 could have been missing John 21:25, the last verse, as is evidenced in ℵ* (a manuscript that has great affinity with 𝔓5), but this only accounts for 102 characters.

the front of the codex. But because Sanders (as with Grenfell and Hunt) believed that 𝔓5 was a copy of the full gospel text, he is forced to suggest an unnatural format for the codex. A more natural format is suggested by a twenty-chapter edition, wherein 𝔓5 had twenty-four sheets and in which the text began on the same page as the title and then ended on the second to the last page (with the last outer page being blank). If the scribe had been trying to fit an entire twenty-one-chapter gospel in the originally designed codex we should see evidence of denser writing, but the leaves displaying John 16 are not denser than those displaying John 1. In fact, John 1:23–31+ has about 690 characters and John 16:22b–30 has 685 characters. Thus, it seems more likely that the scribe was copying a twenty-chapter edition that he knew would fit in the twenty-four-sheet codex. Table 2 shows the two constructions.

𝔓75

𝔓75 is even more likely than 𝔓5 to have contained a twenty-chapter edition of John's Gospel. The Bodmer Papyrus 𝔓75, containing Luke and John, was originally written on thirty-six folios (four pages per folio = 144 pages total). The outer six folios are not extant and the next outermost four folios have large gaps. In other words, the outermost ten folios (twenty pages at the beginning and twenty pages at the end) are not complete (see table 3). According to Martin, who provided a transcription of this text, the original intact manuscript must have included all of Luke and all of John—up to John 21:25. Martin figured that the first twenty pages would have covered Luke 1:1–5:36 and the last twenty pages would have to cover John 13:11–21:25. According to Martin's calculations, Luke 1:1–5:36 has approximately 26,000 characters, while John 13:11–21:25 has approximately 31,000 characters.[2]

My calculations, generated by a computer using the text of UBS[3] (stripped of accent marks), show an even greater difference. Luke 1:1–5:36 has about 27,000 characters, whereas John

---

2. Martin calculated that in N[25] Luke 1:1–5:36 occupies 580 lines × 45 characters per line = 26,100 characters, while John 13:11–21:25 occupies 689 lines × 45 characters per line = 31,005 characters. See Martin and Kasser 1961: 1.11.

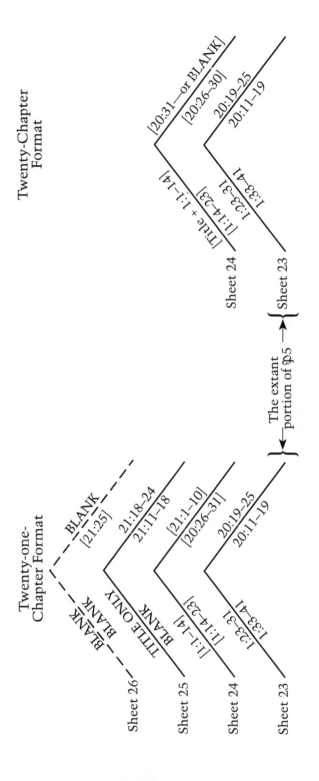

TABLE 2. *The Construction of* 𝔓5 (sheets are numbered backward)

26,500 characters

Folios			Leaves			Folios
1	not extant		1	not extant		72
2	not extant		2	not extant		71
3	not extant		3	not extant		70
4	not extant		4	not extant		69
5	not extant		5	not extant		68
6	not extant		6	not extant		67
7	Luke 3:18–22	3:33–4:2	7	not extant		66
8	not extant		8	not extant		65
9	Luke 4:34–42	4:43–5:10	9	John 14:8–26	14:26–15:8	64
10	not extant		10	not extant		63
11	Luke 5:37–6:4	6:10–15	11	John 12:33–47	12:47–13:10	62
12	Luke 6:16–28	6:28–40	12	John 12:3–19	12:19–33	61
13	Luke 6:40–49	6:49–7:9	13	John 11:33–45	11:48–57	60
14	Luke 7:9–21	7:21–32	14	John 11:2–19	11:19–33	59
15	Luke 7:35–43	7:45–8:5	15	John 10:14–29	10:29–11:2	58
16	Luke 8:5–16	8:16–28	16	John 9:22–40	9:40–10:14	57
17	Luke 8:28–39	8:39–52	17	John 8:52–9:8	9:8–22	56
18	Luke 8:52–9:10	9:10–22	18	John 8:22–38	8:38–52	55
19	Luke 9:22–33	9:33–44	19	John 7:32–49	7:49–8:22	54
20	Luke 9:44–57	9:57–10:8	20	John 6:71–7:17	7:17–32	53
21	Luke 10:8–20	10:20–32	21	John 6:38–54	6:54–71	52
22	Luke 10:32–11:1	11:1–13	22	John 6:7–22	6:22–38	51
23	Luke 11:13–24	11:24–34	23	John 5:23–37	5:37–6:7	50
24	Luke 11:34–46	11:46–12:3	24	John 4:46–5:9	5:9–23	49
25	Luke 12:3–13	12:13–27	25	John 4:14–30	4:31–46	48
26	Luke 12:27–39	12:39–53	26	John 3:19–34	3:34–4:14	47
27	Luke 12:53–13:4	13:4–16	27	John 2:12–3:3	3:3–19	46
28	Luke 13:16–27	13:28–14:3	28	John 1:33–48	1:48–2:12	45
29	Luke 14:3–14	14:14–26	29	Luke 24:51; John 1:1–16	1:16–33	44
30	Luke 14:26–15:3	15:3–16	30	Luke 24:15–31	24:31–50	43
31	Luke 15:16–29	15:29–16:9	31	Luke 23:35–53	23:53–24:15	42
32	Luke 16:9–21	16:21–17:2	32	Luke 23:2–18	23:18–35	41
33	Luke 17:3–15	17:19–29	33	Luke 22:37–56	22:56–23:2	40
34	Luke 17:29–18:6	18:6–18	34	Luke 22:4–21	22:21–37	39
35	not extant		35	not extant		38
36	not extant		36	not extant		37

29,300 characters—for 20 chapters

32,300 characters—for 21 chapters

TABLE 3. *Reconstruction of 𝔓75 (adapted from Martin and Kasser 1961: 1.12)*

13:11–21:25 has about 32,800 characters. When the *nomina sacra* are accounted for, we could subtract about 500 characters from each portion. This would mean that the Lukan portion in 𝔓75 would have been about 26,500 characters and the Johannine portion about 32,300. This difference of 5,800 characters has to be accounted for! Martin says that the scribe made up for the difference by writing more densely as he went (Martin and Kasser 1961: 1.11). E. G. Turner (1977: 74) makes the same observation:

> There are not wanting examples also to show that a scribe, as he made progress with his copying, began to think that he would not succeed in getting his last pages in. In P. Bodmer xiv/xv Luke and John (𝔓75) the scribe makes his writing progressively smaller—and does succeed in getting home. The eye observes the change; quantitatively the change consists in getting more letters into the line. Page 3 (modern pagination) contains 39 lines to a page, averaging 24/25 letters to the line; p. 26 has 44 lines, but still averaging 24/25 letters; p. 98 has 43 lines, with an average of well over 30 letters to the line.

Turner's observations are certainly true. The scribe of 𝔓75 saw that he was running out of room and then began to write smaller. In the first half of the codex, the scribe averaged 40.8 lines per page, 28 characters per line. In the second half of the book, the scribe averaged 42.8 lines per page, about 30–31 characters per line. This shows that the scribe was writing more densely as he went. However, by the time he had come to John 13:10, he still had to squeeze in another 32,000 characters on twenty pages. (Neither Martin nor Turner note this.) This would mean that he would have to write 1,600 characters per page—which equals 49 lines, 33 characters per line (on the average). It would be inconceivable that the scribe would have done this! In fact, there is evidence to the contrary. On the ninth outermost folio, John 14:8–26 is extant. On this page the scribe wrote very tightly—but he was able to fit only 1,350 characters on the page. Assuming this rate for all the last twenty pages, the total is 27,000 characters—which is 5,000 less than is needed to complete a gospel of twenty-one chapters. (John 21 has about 2,700 characters.)

Thus, it is far more likely that the scribe of 𝔓75 was reproducing a gospel of twenty chapters. This would mean that he would have to fit 29,300 characters in the last twenty pages—which equals 1,465 characters per page (or 44 lines per page, 33 characters per line). This figure is far more reasonable and indicative of what can be observed in the manuscript as a whole. It is apparent that the scribe—even by the time he reached John 14:6—was not frantically trying to squeeze many more characters or many more lines on every page. For example, some of the lettering on the pages in the middle of the second half of the manuscript is quite open (e.g., the pages containing John 10–11). As a professional scribe, he gauged his allotted space and then set about to complete his task within that limit. A gospel of twenty-one chapters would have gone way beyond this limit—it would have required at least three extra pages (two extra sheets).

As with $\mathfrak{P}$5, it could also be argued that the scribe of $\mathfrak{P}$75 went ahead and added the extra sheets to accommodate a twenty-one-chapter text. But this argument cannot be applied to $\mathfrak{P}$75 because the entire codex was fully arranged and set before the scribe began his work of copying. We know this because the manuscript, which is quite intact, does not display any pagination. For such a large manuscript to be assembled without the aid of pagination indicates that the scribe was very organized. It is possible that the 144-page manuscript was first stitched together—before the scribe even began to copy his text—or it is possible that the codex was first assembled without being stitched and then removed and replaced—sheet by sheet—until the whole was copied. Turner (1977: 74) affirms the latter possibility:

> To keep his sheets in the correct order without help of pagination would have required strict observance of a working routine: for example, only one sheet might have been removed from the bulk at any one time, and after one leaf, front and back, had been copied, it might have been replaced before the next sheet was taken. It would be possible to verify that the sheets were in the correct order for the binder at the moment that the scribe or the corrector collated the copy against its exemplar.

Whether the manuscript was stitched together before the process of transcription or afterward, the scribe would not have added extra sheets to his codex.

All this goes to say that $\mathfrak{P}$75 is more likely to evidence the existence of a twenty-chapter gospel than a twenty-one-chapter gospel. $\mathfrak{P}$75 has been regarded as an extremely accurate copy. Now it can be regarded as an extremely accurate copy of the first edition of John's Gospel.

Two Editions

If, in fact, $\mathfrak{P}$5 or $\mathfrak{P}$75 or both originally contained a gospel with only twenty chapters, this would confirm the view that the

Gospel of John was first published and circulated without the epilogue—and the confirmation would be based on solid textual evidence.

Sometime after the first publication, John added the epilogue and sent forth another publication. The two editions of John's Gospel must have circulated simultaneously until the first was superseded by the second, longer edition. The second edition, containing the epilogue, seems to be the work of the same person who composed the first edition. But there are various opinions about who wrote the twenty-first chapter: (1) it was authored solely by John, the son of Zebedee; (2) it was co-authored by John the apostle and certain members of the Johannine community (such as the Ephesian elders)—this was the view of Clement of Alexandria and the Muratorian Canon; (3) certain members of the Johannine community composed it after the death of the beloved disciple; (4) it and the first twenty chapters were all written by somebody other than John. I believe John the apostle wrote the first twenty chapters; then later in his life, with the assistance of certain members of his community, he appended another chapter, wherein he clarified the rumor that he would not die before the Lord's return (21:22–23). And I believe that 𝔓5 and 𝔓75, if both in fact originally contained only twenty chapters, provide textual evidence of the earliest edition before it was superseded by the second edition.

The evidence for an early, twenty-chapter edition seems more certain for 𝔓75 than for 𝔓5. Given this and the fact that 𝔓75 is acclaimed for its textual fidelity, it could be argued that 𝔓75 is not only the best copy of John's Gospel but the best copy of the earliest edition of John's Gospel. This should cause us to reconsider the date of 𝔓75. Perhaps 175 is too late. 𝔓75 might be earlier than 𝔓66 (which is dated 150–175), a manuscript that has all twenty-one chapters of John's Gospel; or 𝔓75 (if dated later than 𝔓66) may be simply a copy of an earlier exemplar.[3]

Presuming that 𝔓75 (and perhaps 𝔓5) represent copies of the

3. Some might argue, however, that it seems odd that two manuscripts of John found (presumably) in the remains of the same church library would have two different editions of John's Gospel. Yet it must be remembered that the copyist of 𝔓66, even when he corrected his manuscript some 450 times, did not correct his text according to 𝔓75. In short, 𝔓66 and 𝔓75 were not collated against one another, even though they may have been in the same collection.

first edition of John, we need to ask what impact this might have on textual criticism. Do 𝔓5 and 𝔓75 have a purer text than other manuscripts? Are there readings in these manuscripts that represent the earliest text of the Gospel?

In the portion that is extant for both 𝔓5 and 𝔓75, namely John 1:23–40, there is only one textual difference of any significance—namely the reading of ἐκλεκτός (𝔓5[vid]) vs. υἱός in 1:34 (𝔓75). The reading in 𝔓5 is debated because the manuscript shows only the final sigma, which could be the final sigma of ἐκλεκτός (which according to Grenfell and Hunt 1898–: 2.7 fills the preceding lacuna) or υἱός. If ἐκλεκτός is the original reading, preserved in 𝔓5 (and later in ℵ), then υἱός in 𝔓75 represents the earliest deviation. If υἱός is the original reading, preserved in 𝔓75 (as well as in 𝔓66, B, etc.), then ἐκλεκτός in 𝔓5 represents the earliest deviation. Internal considerations favor ἐκλεκτός over υἱός. Gordon Fee (1979: 431–32) thinks an orthodox scribe of the second century might have sensed "the possibility that the designation 'Chosen One' might be used to support adoptionism, and so alter[ed] it for orthodox reasons." Furthermore, it has been urged by James Williams (1974) that the title *Chosen One* adds one more messianic title to the chain of witnesses in John 1, while *Son* is repetitive (see 1:14, 49). On internal grounds, it would appear that 𝔓5 has the earlier reading and that 𝔓75 represents an early second-century change. The external arguments, as noted before, are more complicated—especially if only 𝔓75 (and not 𝔓5) is a copy of the twenty-one-chapter edition.

If both manuscripts had more extant text in common we would be able to tell more about their textual affinities. In John 1:23–40, they are nearly identical—but it must be admitted that in this portion, 𝔓5 and 𝔓75 are almost as identical with 𝔓66, ℵ, and B. And since we know that 𝔓5 has more affinity with ℵ than B and that 𝔓75 is a precursor to B, it is likely that 𝔓5 and 𝔓75 had their differences just as ℵ and B have their differences. Of course, all manuscripts are subject to textual tampering—whether a copy of the first (and earlier) edition or a second edition. Aside from John 1:34, where it seems to have a secondary reading, 𝔓75 represents a copy of an earlier edition.

SELECT
BIBLIOGRAPHY

Abbott, Edwin A.

1906   *Johannine Grammar.* Diatessarica 6. London: Black.

Aland, Barbara

1989   "Die Münsteraner Arbeit am Text des Neuen Testaments und ihr Beitrag für die frühe Überlieferung des 2. Jahrhunderts: Eine methodologische Betrachtung." Pp. 55–70 in *Gospel Traditions in the Second Century: Origins, Recensions, Text, and Transmission.* Edited by William L. Peterson. Christianity and Judaism in Antiquity 3. Notre Dame, Ind.: University of Notre Dame Press.

Aland, Kurt

1965   "The Significance of the Papyri for Progress in New Testament Research." Pp. 325–46 in *The Bible in Modern Scholarship: Papers Read at the One Hundredth Meeting of the Society of Biblical Literature, December 28–30, 1964.* Edited by J. Philip Hyatt. Nashville: Abingdon.

1979   "The Twentieth-Century Interlude in New Testament Textual Criticism" [article in German]. Pp. 1–14 in *Text and Interpretation: Studies in the New Testament Presented to Matthew Black.* Edited by Ernest Best and Robert M. Wilson. Cambidge: Cambridge University Press.

1981   "Der neue 'Standard-Text' in seinem Verhältnis zu den frühen Papyri und Majuskeln." Pp. 257–75 in *New Testament Textual Criticism: Its Significance for Exegesis:*

167

          Essays in Honour of Bruce M. Metzger. Edited by Eldon J.
          Epp and Gordon D. Fee. Oxford: Clarendon.

1986   "Der Text des Johannes-Evangeliums im 2. Jahrhundert."
          Pp. 1–10 in *Studien zum Text und zur Ethik des Neuen
          Testaments.* Edited by Wolfgang Schrage. Beihefte zur
          Zeitschrift für Neutestamentliche Wissenschaft 47. Berlin:
          de Gruyter.

1987   "The Text of the Church?" *Trinity Journal* 8:131–44.

Aland, Kurt, and Barbara Aland

1987   *The Text of the New Testament: An Introduction to the
          Critical Editions and to the Theory and Practice of Mod-
          ern Textual Criticism.* Translated by Erroll F. Rhodes.
          Grand Rapids: Eerdmans/Leiden: Brill.

Alford, Henry

1871   *The Greek Testament,* vol. 4: *Hebrews–Revelation.* 4th
          edition. London: Rivingtons/Cambridge: Deighton, Bell.

1874   "Prolegomena." Pp. 1–155 in *The Greek Testament,* vol.
          1: *The Four Gospels.* 7th edition. London: Rivingtons/
          Cambridge: Deighton, Bell.

Anonymous

1974   "Lucianic Text." P. 607 in *The New International Dictio-
          nary of the Christian Church.* Edited by James D. Douglas.
          Grand Rapids: Zondervan.

Ayuso, Teófilo

1935   "¿Texto Cesariense o Precesariense? Su Realidad y su
          Trascendencia en la Critica Textual del Neuvo Testa-
          mento." *Biblica* 16:369–415.

Bell, Harold I.

1937   *Recent Discoveries of Biblical Papyri.* Oxford: Clarendon.

1948   *Egypt from Alexander the Great to the Arab Conquest: A
          Study in the Diffusion and Decay of Hellenism.* Gregynog
          Lectures 1946. Oxford: Clarendon.

1953   *Cults and Creeds in Graeco-Roman Egypt.* Forwood Lec-
          tures 1952. Liverpool: Liverpool University Press. Re-
          printed Chicago: Ares, 1975.

Birdsall, J. Neville

1970   "The New Testament Text." Pp. 308–77 in *The Cam-
          bridge History of the Bible,* vol. 1: *From the Beginnings to
          Jerome.* Edited by Peter R. Ackroyd and Christopher F.
          Evans. Cambridge: Cambridge University Press.

Bratcher, Robert G.

1983   *A Translator's Guide to Paul's Second Letter to the Corinthians.* Helps for Translators. London/New York: United Bible Societies.

Brown, Raymond E.

1966   *The Gospel according to John (i–xii): Introduction, Translation, and Notes.* Anchor Bible 29. Garden City, N.Y.: Doubleday.

Bruce, Frederick F.

1968   *This Is That: The New Testament Development of Some Old Testament Themes.* Exeter: Paternoster. American edition: *The New Testament Development of Old Testament Themes.* Grand Rapids: Eerdmans, 1969.

1988   *The Canon of Scripture.* Downers Grove, Ill.: InterVarsity.

Carson, D. A.

1984   "Matthew." Pp. 1–599 in *The Expositor's Bible Commentary,* vol. 8. Edited by Frank E. Gaebelein. Grand Rapids: Zondervan.

1991   *The Gospel according to John.* Grand Rapids: Eerdmans/ Leicester: Inter-Varsity.

Clark, Kenneth W.

1937   *A Descriptive Catalogue of Greek New Testament Manuscripts in America.* Chicago: University of Chicago Press.

1966   "The Theological Relevance of Textual Variation in Current Criticism of the Greek New Testament." *Journal of Biblical Literature* 85:1–16. Reprinted on pp. 104–19 in his *The Gentile Bias and Other Essays.* Edited by John L. Sharpe III. Novum Testamentum Supplement 54. Leiden: Brill, 1980.

Colwell, Ernest C.

1965   "Scribal Habits in Early Papyri: A Study in the Corruption of the Text." Pp. 370–89 in *The Bible in Modern Scholarship: Papers Read at the One Hundredth Meeting of the Society of Biblical Literature, December 28–30, 1964.* Edited by J. Philip Hyatt. Nashville: Abingdon. Reprinted as "Method in Evaluating Scribal Habits: A Study of 𝔓45, 𝔓66, 𝔓75." Pp. 106–24 in his *Studies in Methodology in Textual Criticism of the New Testament.* New Testament Tools and Studies 9. Leiden: Brill/Grand Rapids: Eerdmans, 1969.

1968   "Hort Redivivus: A Plea and a Program." Pp. 131–55 in *Transitions in Biblical Scholarship.* Edited by J. Coert

Rylaarsdam. Essays in Divinity 6. Chicago: University of Chicago Press. Reprinted on pp. 148–71 in his *Studies in Methodology in Textual Criticism of the New Testament.* New Testament Tools and Studies 9. Leiden: Brill/Grand Rapids: Eerdmans, 1969.

Comfort, Philip W.

1989   "The Pericope of the Adulteress [John 7:53–8:11]." *Bible Translator* 40:145–47.

1990a   *Early Manuscripts and Modern Translations of the New Testament.* Wheaton: Tyndale.

1990b   "The Greek Text of the Gospel of John according to the Early Papyri (as Compared to Nestle–Aland's *Novum Testamentum Graece,* 26th edition—NA[26])." *New Testament Studies* 36:625–29.

1991   *The Complete Guide to Bible Versions.* Wheaton: Tyndale.

Deissmann, Adolf

1927   *Light from the Ancient East: The New Testament Illustrated by Recently Discovered Texts of the Graeco-Roman World.* Translated by Lionel R. M. Strachan. 2d edition. London: Hodder & Stoughton. Reprinted Grand Rapids: Baker, 1978.

Edwards, Sarah A.

1974   "𝔓75 and B in John: A Study in the History of the Text." Ph.D. thesis, Hartford Seminary Foundation.

Epp, Eldon J.

1974   "The Twentieth-Century Interlude in New Testament Textual Criticism." *Journal of Biblical Literature* 93: 386–414.

1980   "A Continuing Interlude in New Testament Textual Criticism?" *Harvard Theological Review* 73:131–51.

1989a   "The Significance of the Papyri for Determining the Nature of the New Testament Text in the Second Century: A Dynamic View of Textual Transmission." Pp. 71–103 in *Gospel Traditions in the Second Century: Origins, Recensions, Text, and Transmission.* Edited by William L. Peterson. Christianity and Judaism in Antiquity 3. Notre Dame, Ind.: University of Notre Dame Press.

1989b   "Textual Criticism." Pp. 75–126 in *The New Testament and Its Modern Interpreters.* Edited by Eldon J. Epp and George W. MacRae. The Bible and Its Modern Interpreters 3. Philadelphia: Fortress/Atlanta: Scholars Press.

Fee, Gordon D.

  1965   "The Corrections of Papyrus Bodmer II and Early Textual
           Transmission." *Novum Testamentum* 7:247–57.

  1968   *Papyrus Bodmer II (𝔓66): Its Textual Relationships and
           Scribal Characteristics.* Studies and Documents 34. Salt
           Lake City: University of Utah Press.

  1974   "𝔓75, 𝔓66, and Origen: The Myth of Early Textual Recen-
           sion in Alexandria." Pp. 19–45 in *New Dimensions in New
           Testament Study.* Edited by Richard N. Longenecker and
           Merrill C. Tenney. Grand Rapids: Zondervan.

  1979   "The Textual Criticism of the New Testament." Pp.
           419–33 in *The Expositor's Bible Commentary,* vol. 1:
           Introductory Articles. Edited by Frank E. Gaebelein. Grand
           Rapids: Zondervan.

  1987   *The First Epistle to the Corinthians.* New International
           Commentary on the New Testament. Grand Rapids: Eerd-
           mans.

Frend, William H. C.

  1984   *The Rise of Christianity.* Philadelphia: Fortress.

Goodspeed, Edgar J.

  1954   "Was Theophilus Luke's Publisher?" *Journal of Biblical
           Literature* 73:84.

Grant, Michael

  1982   *From Alexander to Cleopatra: The Hellenistic World.* New
           York: Scribner.

Grant, Robert M.

  1963   *A Historical Introduction to the New Testament.* New
           York: Harper & Row.

Grenfell, Bernard P.

  1897   "Oxyrhynchus and Its Papyri." *Egyptian Exploration Fund:
           Archaeological Report* 1896–97: 1–12.

Grenfell, Bernard P., and Arthur S. Hunt

  1898–   *The Oxyrhynchus Papyri.* 57 vols. to date. London: Egypt
           Exploration Fund (later Egypt Exploration Society).

  1906   "Excavations at Oxyrhynchus." *Egyptian Exploration
           Fund: Archaeological Report* 1905–6: 8–16.

Griggs, C. Wilfred

  1990   *Early Egyptian Christianity: From Its Origins to 451 C.E.*
           Coptic Studies 2. Leiden: Brill.

Hawthorne, Gerald F.

1983   *Philippians*. Word Biblical Commentary 43. Waco, Tex.: Word.

Holmes, Michael W.

1989   "New Testament Textual Criticism." Pp. 53–74 in *Introducing New Testament Interpretation*. Edited by Scot McKnight. Guides to New Testament Exegesis 1. Grand Rapids: Baker.

Hunger, Herbert

1960   "Zur Datierung des Papyrus Bodmer II ($\mathfrak{P}$66)." *Anzieger der Österreichischen Akademie der Wissenschaften, philologisch-historischen Klasse*, 1960/4: 12–23.

Hunt, Arthur S.

1911   *Catalogue of the Greek Papyri in the John Rylands Library, Manchester*, vol. 1: *Literary Texts (Nos. 1–61)*. Manchester: Manchester University Press/London: Quaritch/London: Sherratt & Hughes.

Kelly, John N. D.

1963   *A Commentary on the Pastoral Epistles: I Timothy, II Timothy, Titus*. Harper's New Testament Commentaries. New York: Harper & Row.

Kent, Homer A., Jr.

1978   "Philippians." Pp. 93–159 in *The Expositor's Bible Commentary*, vol. 11. Edited by Frank E. Gaebelein. Grand Rapids: Zondervan.

Kenyon, Frederic G.

1933–58 *The Chester Beatty Biblical Papyri: Descriptions and Texts of Twelve Manuscripts on Papyrus of the Greek Bible*. 8 vols. in 16. London: Walker.

1937   *The Story of the Bible: A Popular Account of How It Came to Us*. New York: Dutton.

1951   *Books and Readers in Ancient Greece and Rome*. 2d edition. Oxford: Clarendon.

1958   *Our Bible and the Ancient Manuscripts*. 5th ed. Revised by A. W. Adams. London: Eyre & Spottiswoode/New York: Harper & Row.

Kilpatrick, George D.

1963   "The Bodmer and Mississippi Collections of Biblical and Christian Texts." *Greek, Roman, and Byzantine Studies* 4:33–47.

Kim, Young K.

1988   "Palaeographic Dating of 𝔓46 to the Later First Century."
        Biblica 69:248–57.

Kubo, Sakae

1965   *𝔓72 and the Codex Vaticanus.* Studies and Documents 27.
        Salt Lake City: University of Utah Press.

Lightfoot, Joseph B.

1891   *Saint Paul's Epistle to the Philippians: A Revised Text
        with Introduction, Notes, and Dissertations.* 6th edition.
        London: Macmillan.

Martin, Ralph P.

1986   *2 Corinthians.* Word Biblical Commentary 40. Waco, Tex.:
        Word.

Martin, Victor, and Rodolphe Kasser

1961   *Papyrus Bodmer XIV–XV,* vol. 1: *XIV: Evangile de Luc
        chap. 3–24;* vol. 2: *XV: Evangile de Jean chap. 1–15.*
        Cologny/Geneva: Bibliotheca Bodmeriana.

Merell, Jean

1938   "Nouveaux Fragments du Papyrus 4." *Revue Biblique*
        47:5–22.

Metzger, Bruce M.

1968   *The Text of the New Testament: Its Transmission, Cor-
        ruption, and Restoration.* 2d edition. Oxford: Oxford Uni-
        versity Press.

1971   *A Textual Commentary on the Greek New Testament.*
        New York: United Bible Societies.

1977   *The Early Versions of the New Testament: Their Origin,
        Transmission, and Limitations.* Oxford: Clarendon.

1991   *The Text of the New Testament: Its Transmission, Cor-
        ruption, and Restoration.* 3d edition. Oxford: Oxford Uni-
        versity Press.

Milne, Herbert J. M., and Theodore C. Skeat

1938   *Scribes and Correctors of the Codex Sinaiticus.* London:
        British Museum.

Morris, Leon

1981   "Hebrews." Pp. 1–158 in *The Expositor's Bible Commen-
        tary,* vol. 12. Edited by Frank E. Gaebelein. Grand Rapids:
        Zondervan.

Moule, Charles F. D.

1962   *The Birth of the New Testament.* Harper's New Testament
        Commentaries. New York: Harper & Row.

Nestle, Eberhard

1901   *Introduction to the Textual Criticism of the Greek New
        Testament.* Translated by William Edie. Edited by Allan
        Menzies. London: Williams & Norgate.

O'Callaghan, José O.

1988   "Verso le Origini del Nuovo Testamento." *La Civilta Cat-
        tolica* 4:269–72.

Parker, Pierson

1956   "Two Editions of John." *Journal of Biblical Literature*
        75:303–14.

Porter, Calvin L.

1962   "Papyrus Bodmer XV (𝔓75) and the Text of Codex Vati-
        canus." *Journal of Biblical Literature* 81:363–76.

1967   "John 9:38–39a: A Liturgical Addition to the Text." *New
        Testament Studies* 13:387–94.

Rhodes, Erroll F.

1968   "The Corrections of Papyrus Bodmer II." *New Testament
        Studies* 14:271–81.

Roberts, Colin H.

1935   *An Unpublished Fragment of the Fourth Gospel in the
        John Rylands Library.* Manchester: Manchester University
        Press. Preprinted from *Bulletin of the John Rylands Library*
        20 (1936): 45–55.

1953   "An Early Papyrus of the First Gospel." *Harvard Theo-
        logical Review* 46:233–37.

1963   *Buried Books in Antiquity.* London: Library Association.

1970   "Books in the Graeco-Roman World and in the New Tes-
        tament." Pp. 48–66 in *The Cambridge History of the Bible,*
        vol. 1: *From the Beginnings to Jerome.* Edited by Peter R.
        Ackroyd and Christopher F. Evans. Cambridge: Cambridge
        University Press.

1979   *Manuscript, Society, and Belief in Early Christian Egypt.*
        Schweich Lectures 1977. London: Oxford University Press
        for the British Academy.

Roberts, Colin H., and Theodore C. Skeat

1987   *The Birth of the Codex.* London: Oxford University Press
        for the British Academy.

Robinson, James M.

1979   "The Discovery of the Nag Hammadi Codices." *Biblical Archaeologist* 42:206–24.

1986   "The Discovering and Marketing of Coptic Manuscripts: The Nag Hammadi Codices and the Bodmer Papyri." Pp. 2–25 in *The Roots of Egyptian Christianity*. Edited by Birger A. Pearson and James E. Goehring. Philadelphia: Fortress.

1990   *The Pachomian Monastic Library at the Chester Beatty Library and Bibliotheque Bodmer*. Occasional Papers 19. Claremont, Calif.: Institute for Antiquity and Christianity.

Roca-Puig, Ramón

1957   *Un Papiro Griego del Evangelio de San Mateo*. Barcelona: Grafos.

Roca-Puig, Ramón, and Colin H. Roberts

1961   "Nueva Publicación del Papiro Número Uno de Barcelona." *Helmantica* 37:1–22.

Royse, James R.

1981   "Scribal Habits in Early Greek New Testament Papyri." Th.D. thesis, Graduate Theological Union.

Ryken, Leland

1992   "Bible as Literature" Pp. 109–48 in *The Origin of the Bible*. Edited by Philip W. Comfort. Wheaton: Tyndale.

Sanders, Henry A.

1935   *A Third-Century Papyrus Codex of the Epistles of Paul*. University of Michigan Studies, Humanistic Series 38. Ann Arbor: University of Michigan Press.

1938   "A Fragment of the Acta Pauli in the Michigan Collection." *Harvard Theological Review* 31:73–90.

Scheil, Vincent

1892   "Archéologie Varia." *Revue Biblique* 1:113–17.

Schmid, Josef

1955–56 *Studien zur Geschichte des griechischen Apokalypse-Textes*. 2 vols. in 3. Munich: Zink.

Schmidt, Carl

1931   "Die neuesten Bibelfunde aus Ägypten." *Zeitschrift für die Neutestamentliche Wissenschaft* 30:285–93.

1933   "Die Evangelienhandschrift der Chester Beatty–Sammlung." *Zeitschrift für die Neutestamentliche Wissenschaft* 32:225–32.

Schofield, Ellwood M.

1936   "The Papyrus Fragments of the Greek New Testament." Ph.D. thesis, Southern Baptist Theological Seminary.

Schwartz, Jacques

1968   "Fragment d'Évangile sur Papyrus [𝔓82]." *Zeitschrift für Papyrologie und Epigraphik* 3:157–58.

1969   "Papyrus et Tradition Manuscrite." *Zeitschrift für Papyrologie und Epigraphik* 4:178–82.

Stevenson, James

1957   *A New Eusebius: Documents Illustrative of the History of the Church to* A.D. *337*. London: SPCK/New York: Macmillan.

Tasker, Randolph V. G.

1964   *The Greek New Testament, Being the Text Translated in the New English Bible, 1961*. Oxford: Oxford University Press/Cambridge: Cambridge University Press.

Testuz, Michel

1959   *Papyrus Bodmer VII–IX: L'Epître de Jude; les Deux Epîtres de Pierre; les Psaumes 33 et 34*. Cologny/Geneva: Bibliotheca Bodmeriana.

Thrall, Margaret

1976   "2 Corinthians 1:2: ἁγιότητι or ἁπλότητι? Pp. 366–72 in *Studies in New Testament Language and Text: Essays in Honour of George D. Kilpatrick on the Occasion of His Sixty-fifth Birthday*. Edited by J. K. Elliott. Novum Testamentum Supplement 44. Leiden: Brill.

Tregelles, Samuel P.

1879   *The Greek New Testament*, vol. 7: *Prolegomena*. Edited by Fenton J. A. Hort and Annesley W. Streane. London: Bagster.

Turner, Eric G.

1956   "Scribes and Scholars of Oxyrhynchus." Pp. 141–46 in *Akten des VIII. Internationalen Kongresses für Papyrologie: Wien 1955*. Mitteilungen aus der Papyrussammlung der Österreichischen Nationalbibliothek (Papyrus Erzherzog Rainer) 5. Vienna: Rohrer.

1968   *Greek Papyri: An Introduction*. Oxford: Clarendon/Princeton: Princeton University Press.

1977   *The Typology of the Early Codex*. [Philadelphia:] University of Pennsylvania Press.

1980   *Greek Papyri: An Introduction.* Paperback edition, with
        supplementary notes. Oxford: Clarendon.

Van Elderen, Bastiaan

1979   "The Nag Hammadi Excavation." *Biblical Archaeologist*
        42:25–31.

Westcott, Brooke F., and Fenton J. A. Hort

1881   *The New Testament in the Original Greek,* vol. 1. New
        York: Harper/London: Macmillan.

1882   *The New Testament in the Original Greek,* vol. 2: *Intro-
        duction, Appendix.* New York: Harper/London: Macmillan
        [1881].

Wikgren, Allen

1967   "Some Problems in Jude 5." Pp. 147–52 in *Studies in the
        History and Text of the New Testament in Honor of Ken-
        neth Willis Clark.* Edited by Boyd L. Daniels and M. Jack
        Suggs. Studies and Documents 29. Salt Lake City: Univer-
        sity of Utah Press.

Williams, James

1974   "Proposed Renderings for Some Johannine Passages." *Bible
        Translator* 25:351–53.

Winter, John G.

1933   *Life and Letters in the Papyri.* Ann Arbor: University of
        Michigan Press.

Zuntz, Günther

1953   *The Text of the Epistles: A Disquisition upon the Corpus
        Paulinum.* Schweich Lectures 1946. London: Oxford Uni-
        versity Press for the British Academy.

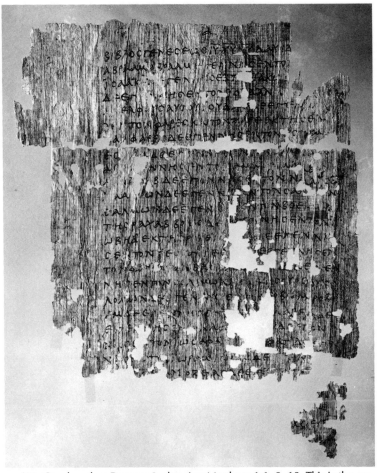

𝔓1. Oxyrhynchus Papyrus 2, showing Matthew 1:1-9, 12. This is the earliest copy of the first chapter of Matthew.

(Courtesy, The University Museum, University of Pennsylvania)

℘5. Oxyrhynchus Papyrus 208, showing on folio one (verso) John 1:23–31 and folio one (recto) John 1:33–40; and on folio two (recto) John 20:11–17 and folio two (verso) John 20:19–20, 22–25. Note line 7 of John 1:33–40, which begins with ΤΟΥ Θ̅Υ̅ (of God). The word prior to this expression could have been ΥΙΟC (Son) or ΕΚΛΕΚΤΟC (Chosen One). One can

barely see the top part of a capital sigma (C) just before TOY ΘΥ but there is not a line over it (the normal signification for a *nomen sacrum* such as ΥC). This and the letter count make ΕΚΛΕΚΤΟC the word that would more naturally fill the lacuna.

𝔓13. Oxyrhynchus Papyrus 657, showing Hebrews 4:2–11 in the left-hand column and Hebrews 4:12–5:5 in the right-hand column.

(Courtesy, The British Library, London)

𝔓46. Chester Beatty Papyrus II, showing Romans 15:30–33, followed immediately by 16:25–27 (the middle of line ten), then followed by 16:1–3. This is the only manuscript where the doxology (16:25–27) appears at the end of Romans 15. Notice how the scribe used slash marks and spaces to indicate stops for oral reading. The slash marks in the doxology (lines 10–20, which ends with AMHN:/) roughly correspond to our modern versification.

(Courtesy, Department of Rare Books and Special Collections, University of Michigan Library)

𝔓66. Bodmer Papyrus II, showing the first page of John's Gospel, with the title ΕΥΑΓΓΕΛΙΟΝ ΚΑΤΑ ΙΩΑΝΝΗΝ (Gospel according to John) followed by John 1:1–14.

(Courtesy, Foundation Bodmer, Geneva)

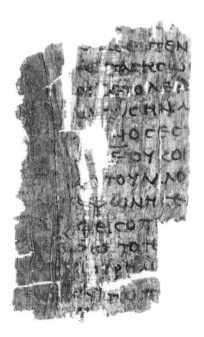

𝔓69. Oxyrhynchus Papyrus 2383, showing Luke 22:41–48 (recto) and Luke 22:58–61 (verso). Note, however, that the recto portion goes from Luke 22:41 to Luke 22:45. The editors of this papyrus were convinced that the only reason to account for this large a lacuna in 𝔓69 is that the copyist's exemplar did not contain Luke 22:43–44, the passage about Jesus sweating drops of blood while in agony in Gethsemane and then being strengthened by angels.

(Courtesy, The Committee of the Egypt Exploration Society)

$\mathfrak{P}$70 (top). Oxyrhynchus Papyrus 2384, showing Matthew 11:26-27 (verso) and Matthew 12:4-5 (recto).

$\mathfrak{P}$71 (bottom). Oxyrhynchus Papyrus 2385, showing Matthew 19:10-11 (recto) and Matthew 19:17-18 (verso).

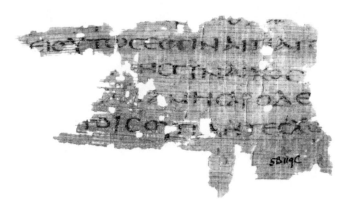

𝔓75. Bodmer Papyrus XIV–XV, showing John 7:49–8:22, lacking John 7:53–8:11, the pericope of the adulteress. In the tenth line John 7:52 ends and 8:12 immediately begins. Note, also the two lines of inverted text at the bottom of the page, which probably reads TON ΥON (or TONΥON) ΩC [K]Υ ΑΠΟ THC TPAПE[ZHC] (or TPAПE[Z|THC]). This enigmatic phrase may mean "the son as master, from the [scriptorium] table" or "stretched/prepared (from τουυον—speaking of preparing the papyri) near ———— [some place name], [bought] from the banker."

𝔓77. Oxyrhynchus Papyrus 2683, showing Matthew 23:30–34, 35–39. This fragment is the earliest extant portion of Matthew (ca. 150). According to C. H. Roberts, it is a fine literary production written in an elegant hand, with "what was or became a standard system of chapter [i.e., paragraph] division, as well as punctuation and breathing marks."

(Courtesy, The Committee of the Egypt Exploration Society)

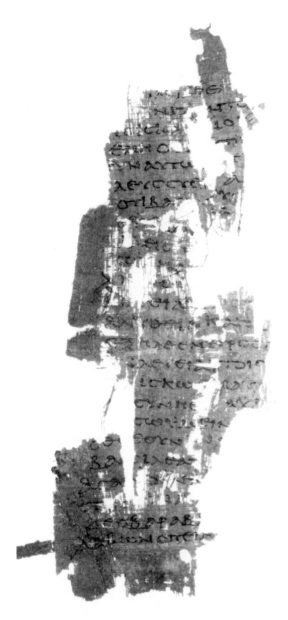

𝔓90. Oxyrhynchus Papyrus 3523, showing John 18:36–19:1 (recto). Note the sixth line of this second-century text. It is the only manuscript that reads [ΒΑΣΙ]ΛΕΥΣ ΣΥ ΕΙ. This reading suggests an emphatic declaration: "A king you are!" All other manuscripts read βασιλεὺς εἶ σύ, which is more suggestive of an interrogative: "Are you a king?"

(Courtesy, The Committee of the Egypt Exploration Society)

189

Author Index

Abbott, E. A., 144, 167
Aland, B., 28, 29–30, 39, 40, 41, 90, 98, 103, 122, 123, 126, 167, 168
Aland, K., 28, 29–30, 34, 39, 40, 41, 67, 90, 103, 122, 123, 126, 146, 167–68
Alford, H., 27, 155, 168
Ayuso, T., 76, 168

Bell, H. I., 35, 36, 168
Bengel, J. A., 27
Bentley, R., 26
Birdsall, J. N., 22, 80, 81, 96 n. 1, 168
Black, M., 123
Bratcher, R. G., 150, 169
Brown, R. E., 146, 169
Bruce, F. F., 24, 77, 105 n. 2, 155, 169

Carson, D. A., 135, 157, 169
Clark, K. W., 20, 169
Coles, R., 64
Colwell, E. C., 40, 75, 92, 98, 169–70
Comfort, P. W., 28 n. 2, 68, 70, 76, 80, 83, 96, 124, 145, 146, 156 n. 3, 170

Deissmann, A., 45, 170

Edwards, S. A., 98–99, 99 n. 3, 170
Elzevir, 25
Epp, E. J., 29, 34, 101–2, 103, 122, 170
Erasmus, D., 25
Eusebius, 13, 24, 36, 36 n. 2, 45, 52, 55, 107, 120

Fee, G. D., 93, 94, 111, 121–22, 142–43, 150, 166, 171
Frend, W. H. C., 13, 15, 36, 171

Goodspeed, E. J., 108, 171
Grant, M., 22, 171
Grant, R. M., 20, 171
Grenfell, B. P., 30, 61–64, 67, 158, 159, 160, 166, 171
Griggs, C. W., 36 n. 2, 171

Hawthorne, G. F., 153, 172
Holmes, M. W., 39, 172
Hort, F. J. A., 27–28, 29, 33, 38, 40, 99, 101, 121, 122, 126, 127, 142, 144, 145, 177
Hunger, H., 32, 92, 172
Hunt, A. S., 30, 61–64, 67, 158, 159, 160, 166, 171, 172

Irenaeus, 45, 47

Kasser, R., 96, 173
Kelly, J. N. D., 50, 172
Kent, H. A., 153, 172
Kenyon, F. G., 49, 53, 56, 68, 72, 73, 74, 76, 77, 78, 81, 104, 172
Kilpatrick, G. D., 74, 86, 95, 172
Kim, Y. K., 30–31, 64, 77, 79 n. 4, 113, 173
Kubo, S., 95–96, 173

Lachmann, K., 27, 33, 38, 126
Leitzmann, H., 57
Lightfoot, J. B., 152–53, 173

Martin, R. P., 150, 173
Martin, V., 75 n. 2, 96, 97, 98, 160, 160 n. 2, 162, 163, 173
Martini, C., 123
Merell, J., 81, 173
Metzger, B. M., 27, 31 n. 1, 35, 68, 74, 79, 103, 120, 123, 136, 137, 139, 140, 141, 142, 145, 148, 149, 150, 152, 155, 173
Mill, J., 26
Milne, H. J. M., 104, 173
Morris, L., 154, 173
Moule, C. F. D., 113, 174

Nestle, Eberhard, 28, 155, 174
Nestle, Erwin, 28

Origen, 119, 120
O'Callaghan, J. O., 30 n. 1, 174

Parker, P., 157, 174
Philo, 50
Porter, C. L., 98, 121, 146, 174

Rhodes, E. F., 93, 174
Roberts, C. H., 15, 31, 42, 43, 47, 48, 49, 49 n. 1, 50, 51, 60, 64, 69, 73 n. 1, 74, 75 n. 2, 78, 82, 82 n. 5, 83, 174, 175
Robinson, J. M., 74, 75 n. 2, 86, 87, 89, 175
Roca-Puig, R., 82, 175
Royse, J. R., 175
Ryken, L., 46, 175

Sanders, H. A., 72, 73, 77, 78, 159–60, 175
Scheil, V., 81, 175

Schmid, J., 81, 118, 175
Schmidt, C., 61, 73, 73 n. 1, 175
Schofield, E. M., 67, 74, 176
Schwartz, J., 64, 176
Scrivener, F. H. A., 26
Skeat, T. C., 48, 49 n. 1, 50, 60, 69, 104, 173, 174
Soden, H. von, 29
Stevenson, J., 15, 57, 176

Tasker, R. V. G., 156, 176
Testuz, M., 95, 176
Thrall, M., 150, 176
Tischendorf, C. von, 26, 27, 29, 33, 38, 126
Tregelles, S. P., 26, 27, 33, 38, 126, 176
Turner, E. G., 37, 49, 57, 59, 60, 61, 69, 74, 74 n. 2, 92, 163, 164, 176–77

Van Elderen, B., 86, 177
Vitelli, G., 64

Westcott, B. F., 27–28, 29, 33, 38, 40, 99, 101, 121, 122, 126, 127, 142, 144, 145, 177
Wettstein, J. J., 26
Wikgren, A., 123, 149, 155, 177
Wilcken, U., 77
Williams, J., 143, 166, 177
Winter, J. G., 14, 177

Zuntz, G., 22, 52, 53, 54, 77, 78, 79–80, 95, 150, 151–52, 177

Manuscript Index

Papyri

𝔓1—20, 21, 32, 51, 53, 57, 62, 64, 65, 67, 68, 69, 104, 106, 123, 130, 179

𝔓4—81–83, 104, 108, 123, 124, 130, 131

𝔓4/64/67—16, 21, 32, 49, 51, 53, 57, 82–83, 105

𝔓5—20, 32, 43, 51, 57, 64, 65, 67, 68, 69, 98, 102, 103, 104, 109–11, 123, 131, 142, 158–60, 164–66, 180–81

𝔓6—110

𝔓8—103, 124, 131

𝔓9—32, 64, 66, 68, 116–17

𝔓10—64, 65, 67, 131

𝔓12—32, 123

𝔓13—16, 32, 43, 57, 64, 66, 68, 68, 69, 70, 77, 77 n. 3, 91, 104, 113–14, 114–15, 124, 125, 132, 153, 182

𝔓15—32, 43, 64, 65, 132, 149

𝔓15/16—49, 57, 63, 68, 112–14

𝔓16—32, 64, 66, 123, 124, 132

𝔓17—43, 57, 60, 63, 64, 66, 68, 114–15, 124

𝔓18—20, 32, 57, 63, 64, 66, 68, 104, 118, 123, 124, 133

𝔓19—64, 65

𝔓20—32, 60, 63, 64, 66, 68, 102, 104, 115, 123, 124, 133

𝔓21—57, 63, 64, 65, 68

𝔓22—20, 32, 60, 63, 64, 65, 67, 68, 104, 109–11, 110, 131

𝔓23—21, 32, 57, 63, 64, 66, 68, 102, 115, 123, 124, 133

𝔓24—57, 63, 64, 66, 67, 68, 118, 124, 133

𝔓26—64, 65

𝔓27—21, 32, 43, 53, 57, 60, 63, 64, 65, 68, 70, 103, 104, 112, 123, 132

𝔓28—32, 63, 64, 65, 68, 109–10, 123, 131

𝔓29—32, 63, 64, 65, 68, 102, 103, 104, 111–12, 120

𝔓30—32, 57, 63, 64, 66, 67, 112, 132, 153

𝔓32—32, 57, 64, 66, 68, 104, 114, 132

𝔓35—21, 32, 64, 65, 103, 104, 106, 123, 131

𝔓36—64, 65

𝔓37—32, 57, 102, 103, 104, 105 n. 3, 106

𝔓38—32, 51, 57, 102, 103, 104, 111–12, 120, 124, 125

𝔓39—21, 32, 51, 57, 64, 65, 68, 69, 104, 109–11, 123, 131

𝔓40—32, 104, 112, 114, 132

𝔓41—111

𝔓45—21, 31, 40, 49, 58, 68, 72, 75–76, 93, 102, 102 n.1, 103, 104, 105, 105 n. 3, 106, 107, 108–9, 109–11, 111–12, 120, 121, 124, 125, 126, 131, 137, 139, 140, 148

𝔓46—16, 21, 30–31, 43, 49, 51, 53, 57, 64, 68, 69, 70, 72, 76–80, 91, 95, 98, 102, 104, 105, 112–14, 114–15, 123, 124, 125, 126, 132, 133, 148, 149, 150, 151, 152, 153, 183

𝔓47—20, 33, 51, 68, 72, 81, 104, 118, 123, 124, 125, 126, 133, 156

193

𝔓48—32, 64, 65, 68, 102, 103, 104, 111–12, 120, 125

𝔓49—33, 104, 112, 124, 132, 152

𝔓50—102, 102, 103, 111–12

𝔓51—43, 64, 65, 112, 151

𝔓52—20, 30, 31, 64, 65, 67, 109–10, 123

𝔓53—21, 33, 57, 103, 104, 106, 111–12

𝔓54—64, 66

𝔓62—130

𝔓64—81–83

𝔓64/67—97, 104, 106, 108, 123, 130, 131

𝔓65—33, 57, 104, 112, 123, 132

𝔓66—20, 32, 43, 51, 57, 68, 75, 83, 87, 89, 92–95, 102, 104, 109–11, 121, 124, 125, 131, 142, 143, 144, 145, 146, 147, 147, 165, 165 n. 3, 166, 184

𝔓67—81–83, 135

𝔓69—20, 33, 43, 57, 64, 65, 68, 103, 141, 185

𝔓70—33, 64, 65, 106, 123, 130, 130, 131, 186

𝔓71—64, 65, 68, 104, 106, 131, 186

𝔓72—21, 33, 57, 86, 87, 95–96, 98, 103, 104, 116–17, 121, 124, 125, 133, 154, 155

𝔓73—131

𝔓74—87, 102, 103, 111–12, 133, 148

𝔓75—16, 21, 32, 40, 43, 49, 51, 53, 57, 68, 75, 87, 89, 91, 94, 95, 96–99, 102, 103, 104, 105, 108–9, 109–11, 121–22, 123, 124, 125, 126, 130, 131, 133, 139, 140, 141, 142, 143, 144, 145, 146, 160–66, 187

𝔓77—21, 31, 51, 53, 57, 64, 65, 68, 69, 70, 104, 106, 131, 188

𝔓78—33, 64, 66, 68, 116–17, 133

𝔓80—33, 110

𝔓81—104, 116, 124, 133, 154

𝔓82—64, 65

𝔓85—64, 66, 68, 104, 118, 133

𝔓86—106, 130

𝔓87—31, 112, 123, 133

𝔓88—20, 107, 131, 136

𝔓90—32, 57, 60, 64, 65, 67, 68, 69, 104, 109–11, 131, 189

𝔓91—20, 43, 102, 103, 104, 112, 120, 131

𝔓92—33, 57, 104, 112–13, 124, 132

𝔓93—57

𝔓95—110

Uncials

ℵ (Sinaiticus)—16, 20, 23, 24, 25, 26, 27, 28, 33, 40, 51, 68, 79, 81, 83, 94, 97, 101, 102, 102 n. 1, 103, 104, 105, 106, 107, 108, 109–11, 111–12, 112, 114, 115, 116–17, 118, 125, 126, 130, 132, 133, 134, 135, 136, 137, 139, 140, 141, 142, 143, 144, 145, 146, 147, 148, 149, 150, 151, 152, 153, 154, 155, 156, 159 n. 1, 166

A (Alexandrinus)—26, 68, 81, 96, 102, 103, 104, 106, 107, 108, 109, 111, 111–12, 112, 116–17, 118, 125, 126, 133, 136, 139, 140, 141, 142, 143, 144, 145, 147, 148, 149, 150, 151, 152, 153, 154, 155, 156

B (Vaticanus)—16, 20, 23, 24, 26, 28, 33, 40, 51, 68, 78–79, 79, 79 n. 4, 80, 83, 91, 94, 95, 96, 97, 98–99, 101, 102, 102 n. 1, 103, 104, 105, 105 n. 2, 106, 107, 108–9, 109–11, 111–12, 112–13, 114, 115, 116–17, 121–22, 125, 126, 130, 131, 132, 133, 134, 135, 136, 137, 139, 140, 141, 142, 143, 144, 145, 146, 147, 148, 149, 150, 151, 152, 153, 154, 155, 166

C (Ephraemi Rescriptus)—26, 27, 27 n. 1, 68, 81, 94, 96, 102, 103, 104, 105, 105 n. 3, 111, 112, 115, 118, 126, 126, 134, 136, 139, 142, 143, 144, 145, 147, 148, 149, 150, 152, 153, 154, 155, 156

D (05)—35, 68, 93, 102, 102 n. 1, 103, 104, 105, 106, 107, 108–9, 111–12, 120–21, 122, 125, 126, 133, 136, 139, 140, 141, 142, 143, 144, 145, 147, 148

D (06)—102, 113, 125, 148, 149, 150, 151, 152, 153

E—148

F (Augiensis)—26, 102, 104, 113, 114, 125, 126

G—102, 104, 113, 114, 125, 126

I—150

L (019)—23, 102, 136, 137, 139, 140, 141, 143, 145, 147

L (020)—155

N—141

P—104, 154

R—141

T—23, 109, 141, 141, 144

W—76, 102, 104, 105, 107, 125, 126, 136, 137, 139, 141, 141, 142, 143, 144, 145, 146, 147

Z—106, 136

Δ—139

Θ—139

Ξ (Zacynthius)—23, 26

Ψ—139

048—153

069—64, 65

071—64, 65

083—142

090—136

0115—139

0124—140, 142

0162—33, 64, 65, 109–10, 123, 131

0163—64, 66

0169—64, 66, 67

0170—141

0171—33, 102, 103, 104, 106, 108–9, 123

0172—64, 65

0173—64, 66

0176—64, 65

0189—32, 103, 111–12, 123, 131

0206—64, 66

0212—33

0220—33, 102, 104, 112, 114, 123, 132

0232—117

Minuscules

*f*1—76, 125, 126, 135

*f*13—125, 126, 136, 139

28—76

33—23, 96, 102, 139, 141, 148, 149, 150, 151, 152, 153, 154, 155

81—102

104—102

326—102

383—102

579—23, 102

614—102

1175—102

1739—23, 79, 80, 102, 104, 112, 115, 148, 149, 150, 151, 152, 153, 154, 155

2344—81

Scripture Index

General comments about the textual character of individual books or groups of books precede specific references and are marked with an asterisk.

Leviticus
15—137

Numbers
12:7—153

Deuteronomy
18:16–18—143

2 Samuel
7:12–14—143

Psalms
2:2—143
2:6—143
2:7—143
78:2—135

Proverbs
8:36—154

Isaiah
8:14–15—136
9:1–2—145
9:6—143
42:1—143
53—143
61—48

Daniel
2:34–35—136
2:44–45—136
7:13—143
9:25—143

Zephaniah
3:15—143

Gospels
*21, 44, 46, 47, 49, 68, 103

Matthew
*19, 20, 65, 104, 105 n. 3, 106–7, 124, 125, 130–31
1:1–9—179
1:12—179
3:7—134
3:16—134
4:24—134–35
5:15—140
5:22—83
5:25—83
5:28—135
9:5—148
9:14—135
11:26–27—186

12:4–5—186
13:35—135
13:56—137
16:2b–3—135–36
19:10–11—186
19:17–18—186
19:19—119
21:44—136
23:30–34—188
23:35–39—188
23:38—70
24:15—44
26:20—76

Mark
*20, 45, 49, 49 n. 1, 55, 65, 76, 104, 105, 107, 124, 125, 131
2:5—136
2:8—139
2:9—136, 148
3:32—136–37
4:21—140
4:21–22—139
5:26—139
6:3—137
6:23—76
7:4—137
8:12—139

10:19—119
13:14—44
14:30—137
14:68—137
14:72—137
16:1–8—138
16:8—137, 138
16:9–20—49 n. 1,
  137–38

Luke
*19, 20, 45, 55, 56, 65,
  104, 108–9, 124, 125,
  131
1:4—56
1:78—83
2:40—139
3:22—83
4:16—44
4:17–20—49
5:23—148
6:1—83
8:16—139
8:16–17—139
8:43—139
10:20—140
10:21—76, 139–40
10:38—76
10:42—76
11:14—76, 140
11:33—140
12:54–56—136
17:24—140–41
18:11—141
18:20—119
20:18—136
20:43—136
21:38—144
22:41–48—185
22:43–44—70, 99,
  141–42, 185
22:58–61—185
23:34—99, 142
24:36—99
24:40—99
24:51—99
24:52—99

John
*19, 20, 45, 55, 65, 94,
  98, 104, 106, 109–11,
  124, 125, 131, 157–66
1:1—143
1:1–14—184
1:14—143, 166
1:17—143
1:18—143
1:19—142
1:23–31—180
1:29—143
1:33–40—180
1:34—70, 142–43, 166
1:36—143
1:41—143
1:45—143
1:49—143, 166
1:51—143
3:11—146
4:1—95, 143
4:11—99
4:35–36—143
4:42—99
4:52—99
5:2—99
5:8—148
5:19—99
5:44—95, 144
7:37–39—145
7:39—93
7:40—93
7:40–52—145
7:42—99
7:43—99
7:46—93
7:49–8:22—187
7:52—144–45, 187
7:53–8:11—95, 144–45,
  187
8:12—144–45, 187
9:4—145–46
9:38—99
9:38–39a—146
10:16—76
10:26—93
10:29—95, 146
11:17—99
11:25—76

11:33—93, 139
11:45—76
13:2—95, 147
13:19—93
13:21—139
13:31—147
13:32—147
14:4—93
18:36–19:1—189
19:35—95, 147
20:11–17—180
20:19–20—180
20:22–25—180
20:31—95, 147–48
21—98, 109, 157–66
21:22–23—165

Acts
*20, 21, 44, 45, 46, 47,
  49, 55, 65, 68, 102–3,
  104, 105, 108,
  111–12, 120–21, 124,
  125, 131
2:10—35
3:6—148
8:25–39—35
11:19—35
13:27—44
13:33—148
15:21—44
17:28—44, 45
18:24–25—35
23:26—108
24:3—108
26:25—108

Pauline Epistles
*20, 21, 45, 46, 47, 49,
  50, 55, 68, 77, 104,
  112–14, 114

Romans
*44, 46, 55, 65, 78, 79,
  113, 124, 125, 131–32
1:7—151
8:9—149
8:21—80
8:27—148

8:28—80, 148–49
8:34—70
9:30–33—136
15:30–33—183
16—77, 113
16:1–3—183
16:23—45
16:25–27—77, 183

1 Corinthians
*65, 78, 113, 124, 125,
    132
1:3—151
1:23—136
5:9—55
7:10—149
7:25—149
7:40—70, 149
10:2—80, 149
10:4—155
10:9—80, 155
13:3—80
14:19—56
14:26—44
15:32—45
15:49—150

2 Corinthians
*78, 113, 124, 125, 132
1–9—113
1:2—151
1:10—80, 150
1:11—150
1:12—80, 150–51
2:1—80
2:4—55
3:9—80
8:2—150
9:11—150
9:13—150
10–13—113
11:3—150

Galatians
*46, 65, 78, 113, 124,
    125, 132
1:3—151
1:15—151

6:6—56
6:11—45

Ephesians
*44, 46, 55, 78, 79, 113,
    124, 125, 132, 151–52
1:1—80, 151–52
1:2—151
1:14—80
3:3–6—44
3:9—80
4:28—80, 152
5:6—153

Philippians
*66, 78, 113, 124, 125,
    132
1:2—151
1:14—80
3:3—152–53
3:13—80

Colossians
*45, 55, 79, 113, 124,
    125, 132
3:4—80
3:6—80, 153
3:16—44
4:16—44, 45, 55, 113
4:18—45

1 Thessalonians
*66, 113, 124, 125, 132
5:9—70, 153
5:27—44

2 Thessalonians
*66, 113, 132
3:17—45

Pastoral Epistles
*19, 20, 46, 113, 114

1–2 Timothy
*45

1 Timothy
1:17—156
4:13—44
6:20—55

2 Timothy
1:12—55
1:14—55
2:2—55
3:15–17—42
4:13—46, 49–50

Titus
*45, 66, 104, 114, 125,
    132
1:12—44

Philemon
*45, 113, 114, 133

General Epistles
*19, 47, 68

Hebrews
*44, 46, 66, 68, 77, 78,
    79, 104, 105 n. 2,
    113, 114–15, 124,
    125, 132
3:2—70, 153
3:5—153
3:6—70, 80
4:2—70, 80
4:2–11—182
4:8—155
4:12–5:5—182
11:11—80
12:3—70, 80, 153–54

James
*46, 66, 68, 104, 115,
    124, 125, 133

Petrine Epistles
*21

1 Peter
*44, 46, 66, 104, 116,
    124, 125, 133
1:11—149
1:22—96
2:21—154
3:14-18—154
3:18—96, 154
5:2—96
5:12—45

2 Peter
*46, 104, 116–17, 124,
    125, 133

1:3—96, 154–55
2:4—96
2:20—96
2:22—95
3:15-16—47

Johannine Epistles
*116–17, 133

1 John
*66

Jude
*21, 46, 116–17, 124,
    125, 133
5—155

Revelation
*19, 20, 26, 44, 46, 47,
    55, 66, 68, 81, 104,
    118, 124, 125, 133
1:3—44
1:4—55
14:3—81, 156
15:3—81, 156